Skills and Methods in

Skills and Methods in Social Work

JOHN HAINES

Senior Lecturer in Social Work
University of Leicester

Constable London

First published in Great Britain 1975
by Constable and Co Ltd
10 Orange Street London WC2H 7EG
Hardback ISBN 0 09 460230 1
Paperback ISBN 0 09 460720 6

Reprinted 1978

Set in Monotype Bembo
Printed in Great Britain by
REDWOOD BURN LIMITED
Trowbridge & Esher

Acknowledgements

This book is based on what I have learned over the years from many different people in the social work profession. I am particularly indebted to those teachers who first introduced me to the mysteries of social work, to colleagues in the profession and in social work education who have provided a constant source of stimulating discussion, and to students in whose training I have participated, ostensibly as teacher but also as learner. I would like to record my special thanks to Alan Jones, who read the manuscript and made many helpful suggestions; and to Clare Smith for her speedy and efficient typing of the manuscript. Above all, my heartfelt appreciation is due to Herschel Prins, who not only read the manuscript in various stages of its preparation and contributed valuable suggestions for improvement, but also through his faith in the project from the start sustained me in the arduous journey to its completion.

Contents

TABLES

Introduction

This book is the result of more than fifteen years of thought, study and practice in social work. As such, it may appear to be a highly personal document, but insofar as it is also based on observation and discussion with social workers in many different kinds of employing agency, as well as with aspiring entrants to the profession undergoing education and training, it can be taken as representative of the state of social work in Britain in the nineteen seventies. The need for a new introductory text on social work is apparent from statements that have been made in the last ten years about its changing nature, most notably in the Seebohm Report[1]* but also elsewhere. The rationale is perhaps most clearly expressed in the words of a Report published by the Community Work Group in 1973[2]: 'There has been a shift from concentration on casework to a new concept of social work, based on ability to assess a social situation and intervene in whatever seems to be the most effective way, whether primarily with the individual, family, group or community or with other social systems.' This basic assumption about social work forms the foundation for this book. Coupled with it is a firmly held conviction that whatever the agency or setting in which they are employed and whatever form their work takes, social workers use common methods and skills, which put together comprise the twin aspects of a purposeful process.

The intention of this book is accordingly to provide a basic introduction to social work which lays emphasis on the generic elements, that is to say those which are common to the practice of all social workers, though more specialised aspects will be

* References begin on p. 213.

mentioned here and there. By 'all social workers' is meant those involved both in fieldwork and in day and residential care, whether as qualified or unqualified staff, trainees or students. The question of who may legitimately regard themselves as social workers is discussed in Chapter 1. For the present, it is sufficient to say that a new model of social work is presented in this book in the hope that the gap between theory and practice will be more effectively bridged than in the past. It is hoped that the model will provide a framework which fits what social workers actually do in practice but may be aware of only intuitively at times, and which will be of use to students on social work courses analysing their own practice as learners. It may also be of use to staff in allied professions, whose work has a social work content, for example health visitors and school counsellors; and to some of the large army of voluntary workers involved in the provision of social welfare services.

It is important to emphasise the introductory nature of this book. Because of this and the attempt to cover an extremely broad canvas, it is inevitable that some issues have received only brief attention, but in such cases the presentation has been designed to stimulate the reader to think further and where possible to engage in discussion with colleagues or fellow students. Those who wish to read more widely will find in the Bibliography a list of books which have been especially influential in the preparation of this text. A further limitation is the impossibility of providing illustrative case material in a text of this length and breadth. Here again, this is in part deliberate in that the intention is to stimulate the reader to apply the model of practice herein contained to his own work and to test its relevance against reality, rather than relying on ready-made examples from the experience of others. In many places, references are made on a general basis to situations which arise frequently in practice and an attempt has been made to link these specifically with different aspects of social work, including residential and day care as well as fieldwork. Once again, as it would be tedious to illustrate each point with references to every setting, the reader is expected to supply his own specific examples where appropriate.

The book is arranged in a sequence of five parts. The first two chapters provide a background to social work practice by examining its basis and its clientele. Chapters 3 and 4 are concerned with the process of social work, a purposeful activity directed towards identified objectives. Chapters 5 to 8 deal with the methods used by social workers and discuss, but also break away from the traditional model of casework, group work, community work and residential work by adopting the alternative concept of strategies of social intervention. Chapters 9 to 12 analyse the skills required by social workers under the headings of relationships, transactions and organisational skills. Finally, there is a chapter in which skills and methods are examined in a professional context.

1

The Basis of Social Work

Social work is a form of human activity, in which certain members of society, paid or voluntary, intervene in the lives of others in order to produce change. The nature of these changes and the methods of intervention they involve are the concern of this book, but first it is necessary to examine various aspects of the phenomenon which is social work, as a foundation for the discussion which follows in subsequent chapters. In this chapter, attempts are made to answer a number of questions. What exactly is social work and how did it originate? With what is it basically concerned? What is its value base? On what knowledge is it founded? Finally, who are those who claim to be its exponents; to whom may the title 'social worker' legitimately be applied?

The Nature of Social Work

The very existence of man in society rather than in isolation involves him in a mutual process of interchange with other human beings. This is essential both to ensure the continuation of the basic necessities of life, such as food, warmth and shelter, and also as part of the process of regulating behaviour that is represented by law and tradition. Although these aims are common to all societies, there are great differences in the means employed to achieve them, ranging from friendly bargaining at one extreme to bloodthirsty conflict at the other. The aims of man in society are also the aims of social work insofar as its central concerns are the basic necessities of life and the regulation of behaviour, but the means employed by its practitioners are influenced by their values and beliefs, which tend to place limits on the methods they use, excluding, for example, warfare and repression. Social work may be said to spring from those means of interaction between human beings designed to bring about change through caring and concern, although many of its practitioners do not entirely rule out certain forms of conflict, as will be seen in subsequent chapters. As such, it has a special interest in those members of society who may be deemed to be disadvantaged in some way, in broad terms those who are handicapped either mentally, physically or socially. In Chapter 2, it is suggested that the social worker's clientèle is now expanding to include the whole of society, but this is by no means a contradiction of the previous statement. Rather is it an endorsement, because it acknowledges that any member of society may become handicapped at some time in life and also that true caring is a mutual responsibility based on the dependence of man on his fellow men.

If a caring attitude is one of the basic necessities for civilised human existence, it may seem curious that society requires a corps of experts to fulfil this function. It is perhaps easier to understand the reasons for the existence of other experts: doctors to study and practise medicine; lawyers to administer and interpret the laws that govern social behaviour; and priests to counsel men about their spiritual needs and responsibilities. Moreover, in addition to using their technical skills, these and other experts frequently fulfil a caring function, that theoretically should make social work redundant. The emergence of social work as an identifiable aspect of the structure of society therefore demands explanation for which it is necessary to examine two inter-related factors. The first is man's apparent failure to resolve the problems of living in society. He has shown himself unable to create conditions in which he and his fellow men can live together harmoniously and happily and instead finds himself having to cope with interpersonal strife, competition and conflict. There are various possible explanations for this, including original sin, a view of man that characterises him as basically bad and selfish, or, perhaps more likely, the reality that harmony and conflict are mutually interdependent and that satisfying human existence requires both. It is true that anthropological studies have shown that societies can exist without conflict, but these are rare, usually small and isolated and also do not appear to produce a need for social workers to intervene. Even for primitive societies, however, life is a struggle, if only in terms of a battle with nature for food, clothing and shelter. As societies become more complex, the battle has extended to include competition between men as well as a basic struggle against the elements. Most societies have found and continue to find it necessary to regulate the conflicts that arise, usually by means of law, but sometimes in more repressive ways through the use of armies or police forces engaging in ad hoc imprisonment and extermination.

It is noticeable, nevertheless, that however repressive or permissive the social structure, man still finds himself with difficulties in his relationships with others. No law can create a satisfactory marriage, any more than a medicine can cure a broken heart. These are problems for the individual to work at and resolve, but the history of the last hundred years has demonstrated that there is a role in society for various experts in human relations, who may be able to relieve mental and emotional suffering and effect personal change by using their own personality and skills. It is important to recognise that not all of these are social workers as such. Some are teachers, some personnel managers, some psychologists and psychiatrists, some doctors, lawyers and priests extending the boundaries of their own professional expertise; while others are voluntary workers, ordinary citizens, neighbours, trying to offer help to fellow human beings in distress. The social worker, however, has emerged as an expert in human relationships, whose primary function is to provide assistance in this area, making good to some extent the inability of individuals to solve their difficulties and enhancing their capacity for self-management where possible.

The emergence of social work began to be apparent in the later years of the nineteenth century and for a long time was linked with the identification of specific needs for which a specialist service was provided. Thus the probation service focused on work with offenders appearing before the courts, and medical social workers (or almoners as they were first known) were concerned with the social aspects of medical care in hospital. Similar specialist services have developed more recently, such as those for children provided under the Children Act, 1948, and those which continue to be pioneered by voluntary associations and societies to deal with specific problems, such as alcoholism and various forms of physical handicap. It is here that the second factor in the emergence of social work becomes apparent, the increasing complexity of society following industrialisation, economic and technical development and consequent urbanisation. It is in countries that have experienced these changes, largely but not entirely in the western world, that the need for social work has most clearly emerged. In some respects its function has been to deal with the social problems resulting from social change and manifested in crime, mental disorder, physical disease and the various other handicaps that seem to be associated with life in a predominantly industrial society. These are problems that human beings are often unable to solve unaided and when they occur on a sufficiently large scale, governments perceive the need to intervene at national level.

Such intervention does not always take the form of a social work service. Indeed, the most significant forms of state intervention have been on a very much larger scale than this, involving legislation that comprehensively represents what in Britain is called the 'welfare state'. Thus, most industrialised countries have found it necessary to make national provision for social security in various forms, such as unemployment benefits, retirement pensions and schemes of additional assistance to those in special need. Similarly, there are various arrangements for free or subsidised medical care and education, together with housing policies that indicate that the state is also concerned about the individual's need for shelter. Some of this legislation has been based on a belief that poverty is the root cause of human distress, which could be markedly alleviated, if not altogether removed, if everyone had sufficient income to meet his needs. It has to be said, however, that legislation has not so far succeeded in eradicating poverty or any other form of social distress, partly because in most societies there are strong structural pressures against the achievement of such an end: just as conflict and harmony appear to be interdependent, so poverty appears to be needed by wealth. It has also to be said that it is now clear that not all forms of human distress are the result of poverty, although that condition may well exacerbate the effect of a social handicap. Thus illness or mental retardation may occur at any level in society, though the consequences for the poor are likely to be worse than for the rich. That, however, is a largely material interpretation of the situation. Social workers are also interested in the emotional implications of human suffering, believing that hardships can in part be alleviated by appreciation and understanding of feelings, together with changes in attitude.

It should be clear from the foregoing discussion that social work concerns itself both with the individual and with society and is particularly interested in the relationship between the two. As such, it is committed to two areas of activity which, though not necessarily mutually exclusive, are at times a source of conflict for the individual social worker. The first commitment of the social worker is to the individual, family, group or community defined in some way as his client. The term 'client' and the ways in which people may become clients are discussed fully in Chapter 2. In the present context, it is sufficient to note that the social worker has a responsibility to provide a helping service to those with whom he works directly. Some may seek his help on their own initiative, others may become known to him because of certain statutory responsibilities he is required to fulfil or because other individuals or departments refer them to him as in need of the specialist help he can provide. In this role, the social worker uses a mixture of conversation, discussion and practical assistance to alleviate suffering and enable people to deal more adequately with whatever is distressing them. In some situations, he may have a more controlling function in attempting to ensure that laws are not broken or that statutory provisions are implemented and this may mean that he is trying to influence the behaviour of others. It is here that work with the individual overlaps into the social worker's second area of activity, which is his responsibility to society as a whole. This has two facets, which may be broadly described as social control and social change.

The social worker is not free to help clients as he wishes. As with any other member of society taking a specific role, he is subject not only to the rule of law but also to certain other constraints that affect the way he works. Some of these constraints spring from the nature of his employment. Thus the probation officer's task is to discourage, not to encourage, the commission of crime; the local authority social worker's task is to promote good standards of child care, not to encourage cruelty and neglect. Few social workers would quarrel with such expectations, but there are other aspects of the work which are less easy to accept. In the course of meeting clients and visiting them in their homes, social workers are faced constantly with circumstances that may be differently interpreted, according to the views and beliefs of the observer. Many of those in government and authority who vote for the resources that enable social workers to be employed take the view that social distress is the responsibility of the individual, who should be helped and encouraged to come to terms with his situation, make the best of it and even improve it. To social workers, this interpretation in terms of individual pathology is acceptable only insofar as it can be clearly established that change in attitude on the part of the client is the only means of alleviating the distress. Thus, a person who has a leg amputated, but in every respect is well cared for and has adequate financial resources for his needs, may nevertheless suffer from depression or develop a grudge against society, the removal of either of which may enable him to lead a much more satisfying life, in spite of his handicap. It is rare, however, for a situation to be as clear-cut as this, it being much more common for there to be an intermingling of material and emotional needs. This means that social workers find themselves assisting clients to adjust to circumstances which in themselves may be undesirable and which are perhaps contributing in large measure to the difficulties experienced. This can happen both in terms of what the client suffers, such as poor housing or inadequate income; and also in terms of what the client needs, the resources in society such as residential accommodation for the elderly or aids for the physically handicapped, to which the social worker may theoretically have access, but which may well be so limited in supply as to be virtually non-existent. In these circumstances, the social worker may feel that by helping clients to accept the conditions in which they live or the lack of resources to help them, he is perpetuating a system of social welfare which should be radically altered, and is thereby delaying the possibility of change. As such, he may see himself as an agent of social control, whose function is to keep the poor, the deprived and the handicapped from causing too much trouble to the rest of society.

Social control is undoubtedly one of the functions of social workers, not only in specific situations such as the supervision of offenders, but also, as has been shown, in the more subtle form of promoting adjustment in clients. Nevertheless, social workers are also concerned about social change. Their work brings them evidence of needs which it is often impossible to satisfy either through individual counselling or through the provision of resources on a local basis. Many of the problems with which social workers grapple appear to have arisen, in part at least, from faults or gaps in legislation and social welfare provision, which can be remedied through parliamentary processes, provided sufficient evidence and support can be mustered. Beyond this, it often appears that there are imbalances and inequalities in the structure of society itself, which create some of the problems encountered by disadvantaged minorities. This produces the argument that social workers should take a leading role in attempting to promote social change, an aim that is more easily discussed than implemented. It can involve the steady reformative work already mentioned, the drip of water on a stone that in the long run produces change. Some social workers, however, regard this as defeatist and believe in exerting pressure for change more urgently. This can be done partly through activities within professional associations, such as the British Association of Social Workers, but attempts may also be made in other ways, such as the lobbying of interested and sympathetic members of parliament and involvement in specialist pressure groups such as the

Child Poverty Action Group or the Claimants' Unions. Some see even this as insufficient and would urge revolution, an appealing theoretical concept but one which in practice does not usually appear to work to the advantage of the socially handicapped. For most of the time, the social worker has to reconcile within himself this 'dual commitment'[1] implied in his role: the commitment to the individual and to society. The very fact of this duality is one of the foundations for the approach to social work outlined in this book. Furthermore, it is only by accepting it and working in both spheres that the aims of social work are likely to be fulfilled in practice.

Values in Social Work

In the foregoing discussion, much was said or implied about the value base of social work, but it may be helpful to add a few further comments. In essence, values in social work spring from the three philosophical foundations of religion, utilitarianism and humanism. Religion, particularly in its Judaeo-Christian form, has played a highly significant part in the history and development of social work in the western world. Some of the early social work agencies were established under religious auspices, such as the Diocesan Councils and the Jewish Board of Guardians. Many of these have continued to exist until the present day, sometimes with changed functions, but still demonstrating the concern for the individual and for social welfare that is central to social work practice. Those social workers who no longer subscribe to a Jewish or Christian ethic have tended to replace it with a humanist version, which, in terms of attitudes to the individual, is very similar. Basically, the values implied by these philosophies place fundamental importance on the dignity and sanctity of human life. Everyone is to be regarded as an individual of worth, whatever his attitudes or behaviour. To this may be added a view that there is in all men a potential for good, by which is meant the ability to act in the interests of others rather than of self and to live as a responsible member of society. There is also the belief that man has the capacity to change, provided that he has sufficient motivation to do so. This is of particular importance in the context of group and community work, in which it is suggested that by acting together people may not only bring about desired changes, but may also experience a consequential development in their own capacities. Finally, the religious ethic lays emphasis on the importance of social justice, and this is one of the foundations for the social worker's concern with redistribution of resources and social change. It also provides a link with the utilitarian view of the greatest good of the greatest number, which has been at the root of much social philosophy and welfare legislation in the present century.

It is easy to provide examples of the impracticability of such values in the face of reality. Thus people who are mentally retarded or physically frail may be in a poor position to develop their capacities and lead satisfying lives. On the other hand, it is common for the abilities of such people to be under-estimated, as those who give them intensive care and attention quickly discover; and whatever their physical or mental condition, it is a basic principle that they should be accorded the same dignity and worth that is given to anyone else. This needs special emphasis in an environment where it is still all too common to separate the needy into deserving and undeserving. To the social worker, all are deserving, albeit in different ways, according to their particular circumstances. This leads to a further aspect of values in social work, which is that the needy and disadvantaged are the concern of all members of society. The problems with which social workers deal arise from a combination of individual and societal causes so that their solution can be said to be equally the responsibility of both. Social workers sometimes feel that they are being used as a paid conscience for society, which thereby absolves itself of any further responsibility for caring for those in need. They cannot accept this view because they believe that all men are involved with each other and that their own special concern with the socially handicapped needs the active support of society as a whole if it is to be effective in making available the necessary skills and resources.

To these generalised values in social work must be added the more personal characteristics of its practitioners. These are represented in part by the motivating forces which lead them to seek a career in helping others. Most social workers are aware that motivation for their work, which offers opportunities not only to help, but to control, manipulate, dominate and generally exercise power over others, is a highly complex and individual matter. They recognise, too, that there are elements of reparation through which they may be seeking to repay a personal or social debt. This means that in part social work satisfies the needs of its practitioners as much as, if not more than those of its clients, a possibility that its critics are quick to emphasise. It seems unlikely, however, that such an allegation can be proved in any conclusive way. What is more important is that social workers should recognise that their own interests are often bound up with those of their clients and treat this as the first step towards self-control and objectivity.

Another criticism of social work in value terms is what is often termed its middle-class bias. Social workers are usually well-educated people, who were born into or have achieved middle-class status. This means that they place great value on thought before action, delayed rather than immediate satisfactions, thrift and a host of other beliefs that, so the argument goes, are alien to the life of most of their clients. There is undoubtedly a great deal of truth in this, which means that social workers need to be careful to set expectations for clients that accord with the latters' life style and systems of belief. It is not, however, an argument that social workers should change their own values or falsely pretend that they share the beliefs of the client, since both stances are sufficiently transparent for clients to see through them. Rather should the social worker be honest with clients about differences in belief, and use this as a basis for constructive discussion about the possibilities for change that exist. Social workers should also take care not to impose their view of life on clients in a belief that their own way is the best for everyone else.

A final point is the extent to which social work may be seen as political. Insofar as their work provides constant indicators of the need for social change, social workers are likely to be aligned with radical rather than reactionary policies. This does not necessarily mean that they have to identify with the views of a particular political party, since there may be more than one which seeks to provide at least some of the remedies they desire. Alternatively, there may be no political party with a satisfactory policy from the point of view of the social worker. What is clear is that social workers cannot ignore politics, since that is not only the means by which they get resources for their work, but also the means by which they may hope to bring about the changes in policy and procedure which they come to believe are desirable. This presupposes that there is an agreed view among social workers about the nature of the changes needed. This happens from time to time, on specific issues, but it is by no means always the case. It has to be accepted that in social work, as in politics, there are often many alternative viewpoints, each with a right to be considered. Thus although social workers may legitimately seek to be active within the political system, this is only one aspect of their wide-ranging responsibilities. For those who are primarily interested in political activity, it is doubtful whether social work is an appropriate career.

The Knowledge Base of Social Work

Besides being founded on values, social work has a firmly rooted knowledge base. In part this has been formed from the accumulated experience of social workers in dealing with the many problems they encounter. This is then transmitted in various forms, such as word of mouth, lecture, paper and book, and increasingly by means of research into practice. This book is founded to a very large extent on what might be called practice knowledge, much of which has not been verified by research but which may nevertheless ring true in the experience of practitioners. Much of the knowledge of which social workers make use, however, is derived from other fields. These include, in particular, law, medicine and the social and behavioural sciences, notably psychology, social administration, sociology and criminology. Such knowledge can sometimes be applied directly to human situations, but more often it forms a background to practise on which the social worker can draw when appropriate, preferably using it in an integrated fashion that does not require distinctions to be made between subject areas. When face to face with a client, for example, it matters little whether a piece of knowledge is sociological or psychological, since it is its relevance to the situation that is important. Moreover, the boundaries between subjects are increasingly being recognised as fluid, with the result that there are often overlapping contributions to be. made to the assessment and solution of a given problem.

There has been considerable controversy about the status of social work as an art or a science. Early practitioners tended to emphasise the former, believing that since every client was a different individual, it required artistic qualities to understand and help each one. Since the early years of the twentieth century, however, the development of the social sciences has led naturally to consideration of the scientific status of social work. Underlying this approach there has often been an assumption or hope that there might be a scientific method which, once discovered and perfected, would be applicable to all types of case and would therefore provide a comprehensive armoury of solutions to social problems. These hopes have yet to be fulfilled and in any case have become less important as social workers have realised that the route to respectability does not lie only through science, as they sometimes appeared to believe. They are perhaps now prepared to accept that their work is a mixture of art and science, in which the truth may be sought in many different ways. The principal contribution of the practitioner is the skilful application of his abilities in the light of all available knowledge, and this links well with the growing interest in phenomenology, which emphasises the importance of the 'here-and-now' in relationships and sees the facts as a dynamic element, constantly subject to change and development. This approach, which has been described as 'interactional social work'[2] focuses on the subjectivity of the client's feelings and suggests that there is more to understanding than knowing. It suggests that truth is not one-dimensional, but rather that there may be many different 'truths' in any situation. The task of the social worker is to work with all of these truths, assessing and evaluating them and intervening to promote a positive outcome, an approach which is analysed at length in the body of this book.

The Social Workers

In the first part of this chapter, it was suggested that there are many people in society who could in part be said to fulfil a social work role. It is customary for professions to attempt to establish clear boundaries for the practice of their arts, which at once exclude the unqualified and uninitiated and protect the interests of those privileged to be members. So far, this has not happened in social work, partly because it has not achieved the same kind of professional status as, for example, medicine or the law, and partly because its nature is so diffuse that many people who are neither trained nor employed in officially designated social work posts may with some justification claim to be social workers. The professional aspects will be discussed further in the final chapter of this book, but it is worth noting that the fact that so many people have a claim to be regarded as social workers may be a consolation as well as a problem. The problem is one of definition: the consolation is that the resources of social work are thereby expanded well beyond what it is possible for those officially employed as social workers to deploy themselves. Much emphasis is now given to community involvement, the participation of volunteers in the provision of services and the promotion of self-help, so it should be a source of delight to social workers that they are not compelled to work in isolation from and unaided by the rest of society.

The question of definition must be resolved in part, however, and for the present this may be done by identifying those who may claim to be social workers by reason of their employment. These may be listed as local authority social workers, some of whom work in hospitals and schools; probation and after-care officers; social workers employed by the many voluntary agencies still active in social welfare, such as Family Service Units, Councils of Social Service, and the National Society for the Prevention of Cruelty to Children; those community and youth workers who see themselves as belonging to the social work profession;

and the vast range of staff working in residential and day centres[3] and clinics, who regard themselves primarily as social workers. This book is not directed exclusively at these groups, but it should be of central interest to them.

2

The Social Worker's Clientèle

Social workers are well aware that without the existence of a clientèle their function in society would cease to have meaning. In this respect they are no different from medical practitioners, lawyers and other professionals, who are equally dependent on their clients, but those who come the way of the social worker are less easily defined in terms of need and the services they require. Moreover, the general public's perception of the role of the social worker is hazy, to say the least, partly through want of knowledge and partly through the profession's own lack of clarity about its aims and functions. The latter have changed considerably in the course of time, as knowledge about human behaviour has increased and as social welfare legislation has made good some of the deficiencies first detected and tackled by social workers, thus freeing them to concentrate on new activities.

At times this flexibility has led to accusations that social workers were inventing new tasks in order to justify their existence. In a candid appraisal of the profession, Wootton[1] argued that the invention of Freudian psychology was a godsend to social workers, who turned to it with relief at a time when social legislation was threatening to invalidate their livelihood. This extreme view failed to recognise adequately that no reform solves all problems. Even if new difficulties are not created as a consequence, a frequent occurrence in a less than perfect society, the removal of one layer of problems generally reveals another of equal complexity underneath. It can be argued convincingly that one of the great strengths of the social work profession is its very flexibility in the face of a wide range of constantly changing tasks.

It is therefore with a background of some uncertainty that this chapter sets out to examine the reasons for the existence of a social work clientèle, its nature and how people come to be identified as belonging to it. First of all, however, it is necessary to discuss the relevance of the term 'client' to the recipients of the ministrations of social workers. 'Client', though much used, is not a popular word with social workers and wherever possible they avoid it. Thus in the sphere of the treatment of offenders, the word 'probationer' has been widely adopted, though the extension of the functions of the probation and after-care service to prisoners and other offenders and the substitution of supervision for probation orders in the under-seventeen age range mean that it is not now applicable to the whole clientèle of the service. Similarly, social workers in hospitals are able to make use of the term 'patient' but may do so less as their integration into local authority social services departments reduces the strength of their identification with medical care.

It is interesting to note that social work itself has produced no suitable term, particularly because for a number of reasons the word 'client' cannot be said to reflect the true nature of the relationship involved. Clients in other situations frequently specify the service they require, as when an architect is commissioned to design a building. They may also make a payment for services rendered and, subject to the conditions of any contract, are free to withdraw from the relationship if they choose to do so. In social work, it is unusual for the client to specify his terms, although in certain forms of community work the balance of power may come near to making this possible. An example of this is the work of the Association of London Housing Estates described by Goetschius,[2] in which the workers acted as resource people, generally called in only when a community group had need of their expertise. For the most part, clients are in varying degrees of subjection to the social worker, pay nothing directly for the services they receive, have no contract (although the probation order can be seen as a form of contract and some social workers are trying to work on a semi-contractual basis by reaching agreement with clients about objectives) and are often not free to withdraw from the relationship. As will be seen in later chapters, none of these factors need vitiate the process of helping the client but they have had a significant influence on the ways in which the role of the social worker has developed and they make it difficult to advance to a situation of relative equality, which some members of the profession would like to achieve. This is the basis for the movement attempting the 'declienting of social work',[3] a popular objective in which clients become workers and the roles of helper and helped are blurred. For the present, however, it seems impossible to replace the word 'client' and its implications with a more appropriate alternative and it will therefore appear frequently in this text.

Origins of the Social Worker's Clientèle

It was suggested in Chapter 1 that social work came into existence as a consequence of industrial and technological changes and their social implications. In particular, the demand for social work services arose because the system of support provided through the family and the local community reached a point where it was no longer adequate to meet specific personal needs. This was a gradual process, made up of the identification of need groups for each of which services were organised separately by voluntary or statutory provision as the case for them became recognised and accepted. Early examples of the creation of services to meet specific needs were the appointment of the first almoner to the Royal Free Hospital, London, in 1895, and the Probation of Offenders Act, 1907, which gave official recognition to social work with lawbreakers that had been developing on a voluntary basis for some thirty years. In the nineteen-thirties, the social welfare needs of the mentally disturbed began to receive the attention of psychiatric social workers, but it was not until after the Second World War that other groups, such as children, the elderly and the physically handicapped acquired their own specific statutory services. This period saw the official abolition of the workhouse, which had for long been the residual service for need groups for whom no alternative arrangements were available.

Social workers were by no means numerous until some years

after the Second World War, and they saw themselves primarily as specialists dealing with defined need groups, rather than as members of a common profession. Lees[4] has shown, however, that even in the 1930s there was interest in achieving common identification, demonstrated in attendance at international conferences and in a vigorous, though abortive attempt to establish a British Federation of Social Workers. The use of the term 'federation' in this context is interesting, since it implies a grouping of specialists who retain their own separate identities, though sharing common concerns. Thus although the idea of a united profession existed in the minds of some social workers as early as the 1930s, most continued to think of themselves as specialists, who co-operated with others dealing with social problems, but who also possessed a distinctive role of their own, which differentiated them as a group.

Advantages and Disadvantages of Specialisation

At first sight, specialisation of the kind that developed in Britain has many attractions. It makes it possible to focus on a given group, whose members may thereby receive more attention than if they were dealt with on a generalist basis, where they would be in competition with other need groups. It encourages the development of a common identification among the suppliers of the service and the growth of expertise. It may also reflect the motivation of social workers, who often have a special interest in working with a particular need group. These are strong arguments for specialisation, but the very separation implied also gives rise to disadvantages. As sociologists have pointed out,[5] separation leads to the labelling of individuals as problems by the use of such terms as 'delinquent', 'schizophrenic' or 'physically handicapped'. Labels are a convenient shorthand method of distinguishing difficulties that afflict humanity: but it is all too easy for them to be used in a simplified or dismissive manner, which fails to take account of individual differences, implies a clear distinction between normal and abnormal, allows the latter to be seen as totally separated from society and distorts their difficulties to fit the category. By drawing attention to individual pathology, it provides comforting explanations of behaviour that is disturbing and difficult to comprehend, at the same time absolving others of any sense of responsibility.

Labelling also fails to take account of the operation of the social system on behaviour. In a social work context, this may lead to neglect of the client's family and social background, so that he is actually dealt with as an isolated individual. There is no doubt that this has happened very often in practice and for a long time it was reinforced by the influence of psychoanalytic theory, which encouraged workers to diagnose and treat client's problems in terms of their individual pathology, often ignoring the influence of environmental factors. The insights provided by psychoanalytic theory are most valuable to social workers, but only when interpreted and applied in the context of their own role, which cannot ignore social influences on behaviour. It is interesting to note that the first social workers in the late nineteenth century were much more aware of the importance of social conditions than some of their more professional successors, although the balance has been redressed in recent years.

Extending the Boundaries

Specialisation cannot be altogether dismissed and is discussed further in Chapter 12. It seems inevitable, however, that the growth in the range of social workers' responsibilities would eventually lead to dissatisfaction with specialisation and an interest in extending the boundaries of social work. The most obvious manifestation was the pressure for a 'family service', which became apparent in the late 1950s and early 1960s. There were several contributory factors in this process. First, social research began to blossom on a large scale after the Second World War and its findings made it impossible to continue the separation of problems into distinctive categories as in the past. Such books as *Family and Kinship in East London* and *The Last Refuge*[6] demonstrated that individual problems usually had family and intergenerational ramifications that treatment in isolation could not hope to resolve and this conclusion has been reinforced by most subsequent research.

Secondly, experiments in the training of social workers led to a much clearer identification of the elements common to different specialisms. The first 'generic' course began experimentally at the London School of Economics in 1954, providing eventually a common basic training for potential child care officers, family caseworkers, almoners and probation officers and leading to the establishment of similar courses in other universities. Specialist training continued to develop alongside the 'generic' courses, but in both types the common elements in social work practice became increasingly predominant. This emphasis on common factors, which usually included field work experience in at least two different settings, produced a new generation of social workers identified with the profession as a whole and interested in a career pattern that would not necessarily be restricted to a single speciality.

The third factor leading to the adoption of a comprehensive approach to human problems was the growth in the number of social workers themselves. In the years immediately after the Second World War, social workers in all services were few in number and even by 1959, the figures had not grown appreciably, as was shown in an official report on local authority health and welfare social workers.[7] This report showed that there were only 1,619 welfare officers and mental welfare officers in Britain. In the same year, there were almost as many probation officers in England and Wales, the total of established officers being 1,502.[8] These relatively small numbers, which were also apparent in other services such as child care and hospital social work, did not, however, mean that staff were able to work in comparative isolation. They were already aware of overlapping between each other's specialisms and gradually began to recognise that the systems by which they were organised no longer reflected the complexity of the problems they were attempting to solve or the needs of the clients concerned. During the 1960s, the number of social workers grew rapidly as employers found more work for them and opportunities for training increased. On its formation in 1971, the British Association of Social Workers was able to claim a membership of some ten thousand, collectively representing the desire for greater unity both in the profession and in practice.

By this time, the work of the practitioners had provided increasing evidence of the need for a change in focus. Family Service Units, a voluntary organisation, paved the way for a comprehensive approach to family problems, while experience in operating the Children Act, 1948, led child care workers to seek an extension of their powers for dealing with children deprived of a normal home life to incorporate preventive work with families considered to be at risk. Work of this kind, which had already begun to develop unofficially, was formally recognised in the Children and Young Persons Act, 1963, but the debate about the need for fundamental changes continued, reaching a climax in the appointment of the Seebohm Committee in 1965, charged with the task of examining the 'organisation and responsibilities of the local authority personal social services in England and Wales, and to consider what changes are desirable to secure an effective family service'.

Changes of Emphasis

Although less radical alternatives were considered in the Report of the Seebohm Committee,[9] published in 1968, the terms of reference left little room for doubt that it would recommend the creation of a new, comprehensive local authority department, charged with a wide range of responsibilities for personal social services. The weight of the evidence received by the Committee favoured such a change and although some of its proposals were omitted from the Local Authority Social Services Act, 1970 (implemented in April, 1971), the spirit of the Seebohm Report has been widely accepted as the guide for the social services of the future. This is important, because the Report covered a great deal more than the question of administrative reorganisation and tried to inspire fresh thinking about personal social services, envisaging a community service, available to all citizens and based on thorough research into needs and the effectiveness of methods of intervention. Some aspects of these proposals will be discussed further on in this chapter.

Concurrent developments in Scotland led a little earlier to the creation of comprehensive social work departments with similar responsibilities to those in England and Wales. More recently the boundaries of local authority departments in England, Wales and Scotland were further extended to include the provision of social work services to the Area Health Authorities created in the 1974 reorganisation of the National Health Service; in contrast, in Northern Ireland, personal social services are linked directly with health services under the aegis of four Area Health and Social Services Boards. Certain exceptions to the comprehensive rule are likely to remain, in that the probation and after-care service is still a separate organisation in England and Wales and in Northern Ireland (but not in Scotland, where its duties are performed by the Departments of Social Work). There are also many voluntary social work agencies whose activities continue to flourish, often with financial assistance from local authorities, which see them as playing a valuable role complementary to that of the statutory services. Finally, it should be noted that in most local authorities, the education welfare service remains within the Education Department.

These continuing divisions of responsibility are less important than changes of emphasis within the new departments. Soon after their creation, it was possible to discern the start of a change in focus towards total community needs as well as the treatment of identified problems as in the past. Thus although deprived children, families at risk or homeless, the mentally disordered and retarded, the physically sick and handicapped and the elderly had still to be catered for under existing legislation, departments began to study community needs as a whole, in order to identify other groups who might require help, as part of an attempt to promote social welfare, a mandatory aspect of the Scottish legislation and implicit in the Seebohm Report. These changes were paralleled in the probation and after-care service by a growth in interest in the environment and the community, partly, but not entirely produced by the prospect of new methods of dealing with offenders without depriving them of their liberty. These changes raise the question of the extent to which it is appropriate to describe the community as the social worker's client. The word 'community' has many meanings and its attachment to other terms has become a popular way of attempting to give credibility and legitimacy to various forms of human activity. Thus educators talk of 'community schools', doctors of 'community medicine' and politicians of 'community politics'. It is doubtful whether the 'community' in these terms has acquired any agreed meaning, even among the professionals who use the term most frequently, and the same is true of the community focus advocated for social workers: unless, and sometimes even if they work in an area as confined as a single street, social workers are involved with many communities. Moreover, communities as such cannot be said to become clients of social workers in the same way as individuals and families. Some of the problems of definition that arise are discussed further in Chapter 5. In the present context it is perhaps most helpful to affirm that community factors are an essential aspect of the environment of social work practice. The social worker needs to be aware of these factors, and to understand and use them. The implications of this view will become clearer as the sources of the social worker's clientèle are examined.

Becoming a Client

The majority of social workers in Britain are employed by statutory services and it follows that much of their clientèle is initially defined for them by law. Social welfare legislation can be seen as an attempt to protect the interests of the weak and handicapped, to supplement or substitute for family and community care and to a lesser extent to promote general well-being. The effect of this is that needs referred to a social worker have first to be assessed to ascertain whether they fit a category for which it is possible to provide a service. In this sense, potential clients may first be required to 'qualify' before help is given. Thus residential care for the elderly is officially provided only for those who can be shown to be unable to look after themselves and have no relatives who can care for them, though in practice the situation may be slightly more flexible. An even more striking example can be found in the treatment of homelessness. In some parts of the country, the law is so strictly interpreted that no assistance is made available until the very point where eviction has taken place and the family concerned is actually without accommodation, even though such a policy may intensify the problems and involve considerable additional expenditure through taking the children into residential care. Other eligibility procedures are still more narrowly defined, so that, for example, probation in its formal sense is restricted to those who have broken the law and been subjected to a legal process that resulted in the making of an appropriate order.

Legislation, then, decrees that certain services should be provided and thereby supplies the basic structure for the social worker's activities. It says little or nothing, however, about quality or standards, nor does it say much about the quantity of resources, whether human or material, required to serve the needs of a given population.

Beside this, legislation is often permissive rather than mandatory, empowering the providers to establish services but not requiring them to do so and this has led to wide variations in the availability of social work help for such groups as the mentally disordered living in the community and the physically sick in hospital. The interpretation of legislation and the establishment of policies are accordingly of fundamental importance in defining the social worker's clientèle and there is a vast range of national and local factors at work in these areas, of which only a few examples can be given.

Influences on Policy

National pressures to improve or increase services and thereby extend the social worker's clientèle come partly from government policy and partly from the activities of members of parliament of all parties, usually supported by a variety of self-help organisations and ginger groups conducting campaigns for improvements in the lot of specific people such as the poor or the mentally disordered. The Government Paper, *Better Services for the Mentally Handicapped,*[10] published in 1971, was a direct result of a review carried out by the Department of Health and Social Security, prompted by a series of scandals in hospitals for the subnormal and the resultant public outrage. The Paper proposed the transfer of responsibility for the care of most mentally retarded people from the health service to local authorities, with consequent implications for the provision of residential accommodation and supporting services on a large scale. Although this did not add substantially to the powers of local authorities (which were already considerable, though often dormant in this sphere), it obliged them to plan a major extension of services and therefore required additional social work personnel, both field and residential, as well as a variety of other staff. In this sense, it could be said that a redefinition of clientèle was involved, particularly as local authorities were expected to assume responsibility for the care of people who had not previously been considered fit to live outside the confines of hospitals.

When the permissive provisions of statute appear to be feebly implemented, members of parliament may take the view that pressure from the appropriate minister will be insufficient to ensure that a service is provided on an adequate scale and accordingly initiate legislation as a remedy. This was the case with the Chronically Sick and Disabled Person's Act, 1970, a private member's achievement emanating from growing concern about the inadequacy of provisions for the increasing number of physically handicapped people in the community. In theory, most of the provisions of this Act could already be fulfilled under existing legislation, but in the view of many there had been a clear failure to do so on the scale required, probably because it did not place sufficiently strong obligations on the authorities concerned. In specifying a range of services for the physically handicapped, such as adaptations to the home, the provision of telephones and television sets, arrangements for holidays and opportunities for educational and recreational activities, the Act could not be said to have created a new clientèle for social workers, since it already existed. Nevertheless, it produced more work and also prompted a redefinition of policy which enabled many more individuals to receive help than in the past. The latter was achieved largely by a somewhat novel provision in the Act, requiring each local authority to publicise its services and to seek out physically handicapped people resident in its area, the implications of which are discussed at the end of this chapter.

The optional nature of much social work provision means that at local level the individual's chance of becoming a client and thereby receiving help varies widely according to residence. In some areas, certain services are not provided at all because of a policy decision by the authority concerned. Thus there are some local authorities that do not act as adoption agencies and some hospitals where there are no social workers. Both of these gaps may well be filled in the future, but the implementation of any new provision remains dependent on sufficient resources becoming available, primarily in the sphere of manpower, which is the most expensive single item in the budgets of social work agencies.

Resources, or rather the lack of resources, play a crucial part in determining the availability of services and the eligibility of the client for help. Parker[11] has shown that all departments concerned with social welfare are permanently afflicted by lack of sufficient resources and are therefore obliged to engage in a series of rationing activities to reduce or control demand. Some of these rationing activities may be less apparent to staff than to potential clients, who may suffer from delay in receiving attention, brusque and officious reception or simply lack of knowledge about the services available from the agency to which they have turned for help. All of these experiences may act as powerful deterrents. Others may result from attempts by staff to establish a systematic approach to the handling of referrals, involving decisions about priorities. Some social services departments have attempted to grade referrals according to need, so that services can be concentrated on the most pressing problems. This may mean that those with a low priority get no service at all, but the alternative might be to spread resources more thinly, thereby satisfying even fewer people.

Another method of rationing is the exclusion of certain clients from help, when it is not obligatory to provide it, in order to offer a better service to others. Thus from time to time, some probation and after-care departments cease to provide a marital counselling service for the general public, though it is still available for those referred by the courts, to whom there is a statutory obligation. While there is no easy answer to the problem of inadequate resources, attempts to be systematic and rational in their allocation are important insofar as they are in the best interests of the majority of clients. Such measures are certainly appropriate as a short-term policy, but their restrictiveness conflicts with the concept of a much wider role for the social worker that has come into prominence in recent years.

Influence of Social Workers

Although law and policy play an important part in the definition of clientèle, social workers themselves also make a major contribution to the process. Their contact with potential clients makes them constantly aware of gaps and inadequacies in existing services and they are often obliged to make extremely difficult decisions about eligibility for help. In some cases, the problems may arise from what appear to be injustices in society, which the social worker has little power to prevent or change, for example, poverty and unemployment, though it may be possible to initiate some mitigation through contact with other agencies, such as the Supplementary Benefits Commission and the Department of Employment. In other cases, eligibility may be established only for the social worker to discover that the necessary resources are not available. Examples of this are the waiting list of elderly people for whom residential care is an established need, although most of them are unlikely to obtain it until they become a 'real' emergency; and on a different level, the adolescents for whom group work would be appropriate if only time, money and a meeting place could be found. In their study of the poverty programme in the United States of America, Marris and Rein[12] showed how easily well-intentioned intervention can lead to increased frustration and resentment, quoting a graphic example of out-of-work young men who were given training for industry only to discover afterwards that no employment was available anyway. Social workers have to be wary of raising false hopes, an uncomfortable and often unpleasant aspect of their role.

The frustrations produced by dealing with so many situations in which their power to help is strictly limited has not been an entirely negative influence, since this has prompted social workers to think about alternative approaches. At the operational level this has led them to develop an interest in working more closely with other agencies, both statutory and voluntary, and in exploring the possibilities of co-operation with volunteers, a growing band of recruits in many agencies, who are often able to provide regular personal attention to one or two clients on a scale impossible for social workers to achieve, because of the general pressure of their much larger workloads. Frustration has also encouraged social workers to take an active interest in the formulation of policy, a process in which they have the potential to play a key role, by reason of their possession of facts about social need, albeit in an unselected and sometimes disorganised form. Social work is a young profession and its rapid development has obliged it to be swayed by demand, instead of being able to control it. Demand, often generated by new legislation, has generally been well ahead of resources, so that social workers have not had time to think and plan on a comprehensive basis. Indeed, they have sometimes been unduly influenced by fashion which has not always produced entirely beneficial results for clients, as the reaction against residential institutions and enthusiasm for foster care following the Children Act, 1948, can now be seen to demonstrate. The assumption that foster care was appropriate for most children deprived of a normal home life held sway for many years until accumulated experience of breakdowns and the findings of research combined to undermine the infallibility of such a doctrinaire view.

A Comprehensive Approach

There are now signs that the definition of clientèle is being approached in a more co-ordinated and rational manner. The Seebohm Report contained a chapter on research and its implications have been taken up with enthusiasm by social services departments, many of which have established data collection systems and evaluation sections. The underlying philosophy here is that it is senseless to provide services unless more is known about the nature of demand and the ways in which it is changing. This approach was carried a stage further in 1972 by the decision of the Secretary of State for Social Services to obtain from all local authorities a ten-year development plan for their personal social services, to be updated periodically. This involves a comprehensive analysis of social need and detailed forecasting of future provision in terms of manpower, buildings and supporting facilities. This is the first official attempt to study social need on such a broad basis and it cannot fail to produce ambitious plans for the future, which will involve a major shift of resources towards the personal social services to make them efficient, effective and comprehensive.

This emphasis on careful thinking and thorough planning, coupled with the growing importance of the concept of promoting social welfare, implies that there may now be a new answer to the question, 'Who is the client?' Social workers have long been aware that the identified client is not necessarily the only person in need of help. The labelling process previously discussed has not prevented them from offering help to the families of 'delinquents', 'schizophrenics', 'deprived' children and many others, where they have perceived that the manifestations of behaviour that initiated their involvement have ramifications that spread into a complex network of relationships. It is natural to develop from this point a process of seeking out clients in order to offer help, as is required by the Chronically Sick and Disabled Persons Act, but also implied in other legislation permitting preventive work, such as the Children and Young Persons Act, 1963. It has already been found by social workers engaged in intermediate treatment activities as envisaged in the Children and Young Persons Act, 1969, that the group work involved attracts the interest of other young people not strictly eligible and as social work adopts a more positive preventive role, this experience is likely to be repeated in other spheres, for example in community service by offenders. The logical implication of this process is for social workers to be concerned with all types of social need, irrespective of strict eligibility, a daunting prospect but one which seems likely to become a central focus in personal social services in the future. It is here that the developing interest in communities is of importance in providing social workers with a local focus that goes much wider than formally identified clientèle.

The social worker of the future will accordingly be expected to give his attention to a defined geographical area, to develop links with local people that will make speedy referrals possible, to work alongside them in the solution of their problems and to put them in touch with outside resources which they do not have readily available themselves. He will still be concerned with individual and family problems but his focus will have broadened to take in the community as a whole and this implies a movement away from the authoritarian and omnipotent roles of the past to a level of participation and mutual support that is already apparent in some community projects, but has yet to permeate statutory services.

3

The Assessment of Social Situations

Outside observers and even clients often view social work as nothing more than a series of well-meaning but otherwise unco-ordinated activities, based more on emotion than on rationality. This is demonstrated in comments like 'I'm sure your work is very valuable but what do you actually do that is different from any ordinary person helping someone else?' The tendency to understand social work in terms of isolated and even erratic helping activities has perhaps been encouraged by the reticence of members of the profession in providing explanations for what they do, a failing which has probably been compounded by their own lack of clarity about the nature of their work. Humility is a highly desirable quality in anyone dealing in personal relationships, but it has negative effects when it raises excessive doubts about the value of the work involved. As a consequence, social workers have sometimes been ready to share the popular view of their work as some kind of enlightened amateurism, ignoring the fact that for much of their working time they are engaging in highly complex activities involving skill and ingenuity.

This chapter and the one that follows are concerned with aspects of the process of social work, which is a more logical way of analysing the highly complex activities involving such skill and ingenuity. A process in this sense is simply a sequence of operations having a beginning, a middle and an end. In practice, it may be very difficult to distinguish these three phases in any one case, particularly when all three are spread over a short space of time. Thus the entire process of social work is sometimes encompassed in one or two interviews, lasting in all for possibly no more than two hours. At the other extreme, there may be a continuing relationship between social worker and client for a period of many years, with the beginning largely forgotten and the end nowhere in sight. Nevertheless, in both of these situations and in all which fall in between, it is still useful and relevant to analyse social work in terms of the process model.

The three phases of the social work process may be identified as assessment, action and evaluation, these corresponding to the beginning, middle and ending stages, but only to the extent that they can be separated for practical purposes. This is an important qualification, since in practice the assessment phase may continue well after the beginning of a case, action may be necessary almost from the start and evaluation is usually an on-going activity throughout. The three phases are also mutually influential in the sense that there is often re-assessment as a consequence of a formal evaluation and this in turn affects the type of action involved. Although it is perhaps easier to apply this model of the social work process to cases that continue for a period of time, it also has relevance for single interview situations, where all three phases are encapsulated in the space of an hour or less; in addition, assessment, action and evaluation can be seen as the three principal strands of every meeting between social worker and client, whether it takes place in isolation or as one of a continuing series.

Meetings between social worker and client are thus not random activities without a purpose. The elements of assessment, action and evaluation imply that there are objectives to be specified and achieved. These may be modified in the light of experience and evaluation but their existence is vital to effective social work, which is a purposeful and goal-directed activity. The remainder of this chapter is concerned with the first phase of the process, that involving assessment. Action and evaluation are discussed in Chapter 4.

Client Meets Worker

Social work begins at the point at which client and worker meet for the first time and this can happen in a variety of ways. In some cases, the client himself initiates the meeting, seeking help which he thinks is likely to be available from the social worker or his employing agency. Thus someone needing assistance with the care of an elderly relative may know enough about welfare provisions to be aware that the social services department of the local authority should be approached. Similarly, men discharged from prison usually know that help is available from the probation and after-care service, should they require it, and they themselves may initiate contact on a voluntary basis. Not all potential clients are as well-informed as these, however, and thus they may seek help but from an agency or department which is not empowered to provide it. One of the first tasks of the social worker in the assessment stage is to discover what kind of help is being sought and then decide whether it is possible for his agency to provide it. If the answer to this is a negative one, then the appropriate course of action is generally to make a speedy referral to whatever department offers the service required. Thus parents concerned about behaviour difficulties of their children may well approach a probation officer because of his association with the courts and the treatment of delinquency, but will probably find that they are referred to the social services department, which nowadays more often deals with the problems of children and potential offenders. (In Scotland, this problem of referral would not arise because, as was indicated in Chapter 2, there is no longer a separate probation and after-care service: even so, the departments of social work do not carry out all the social work in Scotland, there being still many voluntary organisations, so inappropriate referrals are still likely to occur.)

The illustrations given so far might give the impression that it is always a simple matter to decide whether the client fits into a category for which it is possible to provide a service, but that is not always the case. Most social workers are familiar with clients who arrive for no apparent reason and who cannot give a clear account of their problems, let alone any indication of the help they require. In such cases, several meetings may be necessary before a decision can be made about what help is appropriate and whether to refer to another agency. This applies particularly to clients showing signs of mental confusion or suffering from stresses which give the impression that they are disorientated and disordered. Such people may require the expenditure of a great deal of time and patience if their needs are to be accurately assessed and appropriate action taken.

It should now be clear that the labelling process discussed in Chapter 2 is closely related to the way in which social welfare provisions are organised. This means that in order to obtain help, a client must be assessed as belonging to a particular category defined by law or in some cases by procedure and precedent. At the time of the meetings of the Seebohm Committee, there was much talk of the idea of a 'single door on which to knock' and the Committee's Report certainly emphasised the importance of meeting need on a very widely defined basis. For this reason, their interpretation of a 'family service' was extremely broad, the Committee taking the view that as everyone could be said to belong to a family, all should be eligible for help. The reorganisation that followed the Seebohm Report, however, was largely an attempt to integrate existing services previously provided on a separate basis and this has perpetuated the tendency to concentrate on formally defined need categories. This is wholly understandable in view of the demands made by the eligible and in face of severely limited resources, but it means that unless alternatives are available elsewhere, either in the statutory sector or from voluntary organisations, many people may receive no help at all because there is no body or organisation to meet their particular needs.

In these circumstances social workers have three alternatives for dealing with a client to whom his agency has nothing officially to offer. The first is to say frankly that no help can be provided and encourage the client to accept that he must manage alone. This may be effective to the extent that talking to someone relieves the pressure sufficiently to restore the ability to cope (a point discussed fully in Chapter 6), but it is often unsatisfactory, particularly as it may well do no more than ward off more serious problems that will ultimately bring the client or his family into a category eligible for help. Moreover, however realistic it may be for social workers to say to clients that no form of help is available, it is never easy to do this in practice, because it seems uncaring and even callous. For this reason, many social workers try the second alternative, which is to offer help on an unofficial basis. If someone has taken the trouble to seek help, it is an indication that they have reached a fairly desperate situation and may even be going through a serious crisis. In these circumstances, many social workers are prepared to try by listening and discussion to assist the person concerned towards reaching some solution of his own, taking any appropriate action that may appear to be necessary, for example in attempting to persuade other agencies that they should provide help, even if it means making an exception to their usual rules. Even so, an early decision has to be made about whether to refuse help from the start or whether to become involved in work which may only lead to the frustrating conclusion that there is nothing that can be done and that the client must accept this. When time and resources permit, it is arguable that a modicum of help is preferable to immediate refusal, as people who have learned to accept their lot philosophically are more likely to be able to find some positive compensations than those who are weighed down with frustration and anger.

The third alternative in dealing with people for whom there is as yet no organisation to provide help is one that has as yet been underemployed by social workers, but which has great potential for the future. This is the stimulation and support of self-help groups. In the years since the official inception of the 'welfare state', there has been a parallel blossoming of self-help activity to the point where there is a wide range of groups and organisations catering for needs of a specialist kind. Some of these are concerned with medical or psychiatric problems, such as multiple sclerosis societies and the associations for parents of autistic children. Others are community groups such as tenants' and residents' associations. Still others are much more informal groupings of people with a common interest meeting together from time to time. One of the distinguishing characteristics of many of these developments has been the absence of social workers, though it is only fair to say that they too have sometimes taken the initiative in such enterprises as clubs for ex-patients of psychiatric hospitals and prisoners' wives groups. The absence of social workers from many self-help activities can be interpreted as good to the extent that it shows that voluntary initiative is still very much alive and can flourish without stimulation from a professional source. The disadvantage is that such groups are often denied the advice and access to resources that the professional social worker or his department can offer. The increasing powers being given to local authorities, together with broader interpretations of existing powers that social workers can help to promote are encouraging voluntary bodies and self-help groups to enter into closer relationships with statutory departments, which more than ever can provide financial assistance and professional expertise. At the same time, in accordance with the broadened view of their potential clientèle suggested in Chapter 2, social workers have become much more interested in helping community groups to form and develop, without seeking to lead or dominate them. This aspect of statutory social work seems likely to grow as research demonstrates further areas of unmet need and as social workers become more involved in local networks in their attempt to promote the idea of community care.

The examples given so far illustrate ways in which social worker and client may meet, when the latter has in however vague a way perceived a need for help and taken steps to obtain it. Even if the client begins by approaching an inappropriate agency for the help required and is referred elsewhere, this may still be properly regarded as a situation in which the client has taken the initiative. In many circumstances, however, there are other factors at work which influence the client's behaviour. He may be under pressure from friends or relatives to seek help with a problem. He may be advised by a professional person, such as a doctor or solicitor, that his best course of action would be to consult a social worker and the necessary referral may be made on his behalf. Finally, he may be referred for help because people other than himself consider that he has problems or that he is in himself a problem. This latter situation is one familiar to probation officers and others dealing with offenders and also to those whose work involves them in the compulsory admission of patients to psychiatric hospitals. Such cases come at one end of a continuum, at the opposite end of which are the clients who seek help for themselves in the apparent absence of external pressures. The word 'apparent' is used advisedly here, since the distinguishing feature of all clients is that they are subject in varying degrees to pressure, both from within themselves and from other people or environmental factors and it is these pressures that constitute the motivation for seeking help in the first place. The other distinguishing feature of social workers' clients is not that they differ greatly from the rest of humanity in having pressures to cope with (for that is the lot of everyone) but that their innate capacity and accumulated knowledge and experience, together with personal and environmental resources, are inadequate to enable them to deal with life's problems unaided, at any rate for the time being. This may apply as much to an individual wanting help with a personal problem as to a community group seeking improvements in housing conditions.

The Process of Assessment

Whatever the apparent motivation in seeking help and however it is expressed, the social worker's task in assessment is essentially the same: to gather as much information as possible about the situation and form some opinion of its meaning for the client and its implications for action. Adopting a medical model, this part of the social work process has often been referred to as 'diagnosis'. It was embodied in the title of one of the early classics of social work literature, Richmond's *Social Diagnosis*,[1] and more recently has appeared again in Sainsbury's *Social Diagnosis in Casework*.[2] While recognising the relevance of this term, which is fairly precise and well understood even by non-medical people, it cannot justifiably be claimed that social work, like medicine, is concerned with the identification of a disease by means of its symptoms, which is the medical definition of diagnosis. Nor is social work concerned with prescribing in the same way as medicine, although there are parallels in the various types of action proposed by social workers, as will be seen in Chapter 4. Social work is best seen as concerned with accumulating facts, both from the client and, where appropriate, from his family and the environment; with weighing the importance of these facts and their significance to the client; and with calculating the potential for help likely to be available, again in the client's own resources and, where appropriate, in those to be found in the family and the environment. This part of the social work process is more accurately described as 'assessment' than as 'diagnosis'.

For the purposes of discussion, the process of assessment can be divided into four stages: acquisition of information, study, formulation and goal-setting. It is worth noting at this point that this framework has relevance to all situations in which social workers operate, whether with individual clients, families, groups or communities. In all of these, there is the same need to carry out a careful assessment of the problems presented by the client, completing this as early as possible in the process.

Knowledge can always be increased and the acquisition of information is therefore a continuing aspect of social work, but it has special importance at the beginning of any piece of work. In some agencies, such as child guidance clinics, it has become regular practice to begin work on a case by obtaining a comprehensive social history covering the entire life of the child concerned as well as any relevant details about the parents and general family background. Similarly, in social enquiries for the courts, the probation officer or local authority social worker attempts to elucidate as much information as possible about the offender and this is the main focus for the first meetings between them. The need for detailed information has sometimes been questioned, particularly when it delves far back into the past, but it is certainly vital to obtain as much as possible about the present situation and the events that have contributed to it, since this is the starting point for any future work.

The principal informant is generally the client himself and in early meetings the social worker needs to concentrate on encouraging him to reveal as much about himself as will enable a full picture to be drawn of his present situation and problems.

This source of information can often be supplemented by talking with immediate members of the client's family, relatives, friends, teachers, employers, doctors, lawyers and other social workers, who may have relevant contributions to make. It is normal practice to make such enquiries only with the permission of the client concerned. In a group situation, the social worker encourages members to share information about each other, thus enabling him to build up a picture of the needs and problems of the group as a whole. A further source of information lies in the environment from which the client comes. Social workers need to be familiar with the social structure and physical appearance of the areas in which they work, incorporating cultural and sub-cultural data into their assessments. In community work this aspect is of crucial importance and in addition to the information that can be obtained from observation, workers need to make use of a variety of source material such as census reports, electoral registers and statistical and other data in the possession of statutory departments and voluntary bodies. In some situations, it is necessary for the worker to carry out his own surveys in order to obtain the information he requires.

The need for information presents the social worker with one major dilemma. Most people prefer to reveal themselves to others slowly over the course of time as they develop a relationship of confidence. For this reason, they may not at first indicate the true nature of their difficulties, choosing something less important that is in their view more acceptable, as a means of testing out the situation and the social worker. This is the phenomenon usually described as the 'presenting problem'. It is well known both in medicine and social work and it is therefore essential for professionals to be alert to its manifestations. Nevertheless it constitutes a fundamental difficulty in assessment, for a number of reasons. In the first place, it is not always true that more complex problems underlie the presentation of a relatively simple difficulty. This can only be ascertained by sensitive discussion with the client, in which the social worker tries to build up confidence to the point where any more fundamental difficulties that exist can be safely revealed. If this does not occur, it may be that the client is not yet ready to express such difficulties, but the alternative, that no underlying problems exist, should not be ignored. Even if the social worker suspects that there are underlying problems, he may have to be content to work with superficial issues until such time as the client decides to raise other matters. This is not necessarily a disadvantage, however, as the presenting issues, however superficial, may in fact be real problems in need of attention. The conclusion, therefore, is that presenting problems should always be given the attention they require and not be dismissed as irrelevant; but social workers should also be ready to detect clues to other difficulties and make use of the methods to be outlined later in this book to enable clients to reveal them if they are real causes of concern.

A second difficulty about presenting problems is that their expression as the main area of concern often appears to obstruct speedy access to the full facts of the client's situation. Thus although anxiety may impel clients to say a great deal more than they would in normal circumstances, particularly to someone in a professional capacity who stands objectively outside the family relationships or environmental problems that may be the principal arena of their troubles, undue pressure from the social worker may close them up and block the flow of information. This difficulty is exacerbated when the social worker is himself under external pressure, perhaps to produce a social enquiry report for a court or to obtain sufficient information to justify the granting of a rent guarantee for a family that will otherwise be evicted by the local housing department. In these situations, the social worker usually has in mind a list of questions to which he needs clear answers, but simply reciting them in turn may make him seem more like an enquiry agent or investigator than someone trying to be helpful. Fortunately, experience suggests that if social workers begin by presenting themselves in the role of interested helper, most clients produce the information required without being asked directly; and it becomes possible to insert a question here and there in a judicious way that fills the gaps without seeming like an inquisition.

The anxiety to be in possession of facts and information is a pressure that social workers need to control with care. This is a particular problem for students and inexperienced workers, who often take the view that if only they had all the facts, they would both understand the situation and know how to provide an answer. Another aspect of this is the belief that there exists somewhere the truth about a situation which, if discovered, will explain everything. Student social workers dealing with marital problems often say that having seen one partner, they need to see the other, following which the truth of the situation will emerge. The reality is that there are as many 'truths' as there are people in the situation, but therein lies the key for the social worker, for in accepting this, he is recognising that the information he needs lies not only in factual knowledge but also in the way clients feel about their situation. The recognition and systematic recording of feelings often enables the social worker to make do with sparse factual information until the time is appropriate for more to be revealed.

It is important to emphasise here that a great deal of social work is concerned with people's feelings. In work with individuals, this has been a long-established focus, particularly because of the psychiatric influences on social work practice, but although these have now waned to some extent, the need to be aware of and focus on people's feelings is in no way diminished. As an example, it is quite clear that although a person who becomes physically handicapped may benefit from a range of practical provisions designed to make life easier, pleasanter and more comfortable, he may also have feelings of great intensity about his condition, which cause him distress and with which he may need professional help if he is to manage them effectively. The concern with feelings is also relevant in other aspects of social work. Community work offers many instances of this: for example, the initial focus of work on a housing estate or in a new town is often much more on how the residents feel about living there than on the facts of the situation and it is their feelings that may ultimately decide the issues to be tackled.

As the social worker becomes aware of the facts and feelings about a situation, he tries to fit them together in some kind of orderly pattern. He studies each aspect and looks for links with others, a process that may be compared to the early stages of work on a vast jigsaw puzzle. Each piece is scrutinised for colour, pattern and shape and where possible it is fitted together with appropriate corresponding pieces. It is here that the analogy breaks down, because in social work there are no outside pieces with a straight edge, the pieces themselves tend to change colour, pattern and shape in the course of time and in any case the social worker is never in possession of all the pieces. Nevertheless, similar thought processes are involved and it is in studying situations that the social worker needs to exercise his intellectual as well as his imaginative capacities to the full, in order to build up in his own mind something of an integrated picture of each case.

Studying the situation leads logically to the formulation of an assessment. This involves a kind of weighing process, in which positive and negative factors are balanced. The social worker looks in particular for indications of positive strengths, growth points, which may enable the client or client group to move forward in tackling the problems in hand. The strengths include both those of personality, which are likely to be susceptible to reinforcement if suitably nurtured; and those in the environment in the form of other people who may be expected to contribute positively to the process, together with factors in the social system that are likely to have a favourable influence (for example, housing or employment). On the negative side, the social worker takes into account any factors that are likely to inhibit the capacity of the client to solve the problem, both within his own personality and in the environment.

What should emerge is a kind of balance sheet, which for the time being is a comprehensive summary of the situation. Its precise content naturally varies from case to case, but the following examples give a general idea of what is involved. The assessment of a young offender about to appear in court would include his motivation for the offence, his present attitude to it and the likelihood of a repetition; the reactions of his family and the degree to which they would be able to help him avoid subsequent trouble; and the influence of his environment, including his peer-group relationships, particularly as they might affect his future behaviour. In the case of a group of unmarried mothers, the assessment would include not only some estimate of the needs and personalities of each individual member, but also an indication of the strengths and weaknesses of the group and the ways in which it might be used to benefit everyone involved. Finally, in working with a community group, the social worker would assess key figures for their potential both as leaders and as disruptive influences; and would attempt to estimate the balance of power between different groups and the strength of relationships within and between groups.

These examples are necessarily brief and not in themselves exhaustive, but even so they raise an important point about the validity of social assessments. This aspect is concerned with the extent to which they are subjective pieces of guesswork, rather than realistic accounts of the situation. The social worker naturally aims for the latter, but is inevitably aware of the influence of his own subjective opinions, which lead him to interpret data in his own terms rather than in those of the client. He is helped by the fact that he is a trained observer of the social scene, using judgement based on experience. In the early stages of his career, when experience is limited, he may find himself revising his assessments more frequently than later on when he has more accumulated knowledge on which to draw. He may also rightly be more cautious and indeed caution in assessment is a wise course at any time. There is, however, another way in which to test the validity of assessments and that is to share them with the clients concerned, a method which to some extent is used already. For example, some probation officers write a social enquiry report in draft form, which they then discuss with the offender, being prepared to amend it if it seems on reflection to present an inaccurate picture of the situation. Similarly, a community worker may explain to a group with which he is working how the situation seems to him and then invite the members to correct or modify his views, so that together they reach a shared understanding of the problems at issue. It should not be assumed that agreement about an assessment can always be reached, because the views of clients and social workers are not necessarily compatible and the social worker often has responsibilities to other bodies, such as courts and committees that require him to present to them what he believes to be a true account of a situation, whether or not this is accepted by the client or clients concerned. Nevertheless, if effective work is to be done, it is desirable to maximise areas of agreement with the client and to acknowledge differences openly, so that they are then available for discussion and modification.

The sharing of the assessment between social worker and client should thus be regarded as a good principle for all situations where it is possible. It reflects the honesty and integrity which the social work profession regards as fundamental to its existence and it also demonstrates confidence in the ability of clients to accept the reality about themselves, of which many are in any case already aware, however dimly. Finally, it emphasises the fact that the process of social work is a shared activity, a partnership between worker and client in which there should be no unreasonable withholding of anything that may contribute to a healthy and successful outcome. Although there are clients (such as some who are mentally disordered or retarded) who cannot be expected to grasp even basic facts about themselves, social workers perhaps assume too readily that the capacity for comprehension is lacking and thus fail to test its presence adequately. This is particularly important when people are undergoing drastic changes in their life situation, such as going into residential care or coping with bereavement. Although they may sometimes give the appearance of failing to understand what is happening to them, it is vital that social workers give them clear explanations and, in the case of residential care, provide them with information about where they are going. They may not appear to grasp very much, but experience suggests that what social workers say to clients in situations that are emotionally tense often has a significant outcome in terms of attitude and behaviour. Understanding is in fact a highly complex matter, involving the subjectivity of the client as well as the social worker. Leighton[3] has suggested that attempts to be totally objective about situations involving human beings and personal relationships are in effect denials of painful reality. Instead, he advocates 'more precise subjectivity' as part of what he calls the 'act' of understanding. Thus social assessment should be seen as dynamic rather than static, a continuing part of the social work process involving every aspect of the relationship between the social worker and his clients.

Goal Setting

Sharing in the formulation of assessments has an obvious parallel in the area of goal setting. If it is accepted that social work is a purposeful activity, then it must in consequence establish goals both in general and in individual case situations. Much of the social work that goes under the name 'supportive' has been notable in the past for the apparent absence of goals. Clients have been visited regularly over a period of time until the point is reached when the original reason for intervention is forgotten and the visits continue on a routine basis without either worker or client being sure why they meet. This is particularly likely to happen where there is a statutory requirement (such as in a probation order or a fostering situation), which necessitates regular meetings. If the purpose of these meetings is not to be ignored and if social work activity in general is to be seen by clients as having more than a vague and slightly unpleasant meaning, it is vital for goals to be formulated on an agreed basis. That this is possible has been shown in work carried out in the sphere of behaviour modification (discussed in Chapter 7), in which, with the agreement of the client, clear goals are formulated and these become the focus of treatment. Similar attempts to clarify problems and formulate goals are characteristic of what is known as 'task-centred casework', an approach in which there is considerable emphasis on client-participation in the process.[4] Thus clients are themselves expected to do a great deal of work on resolving their problems, which are in any case tackled on a selective basis. The social worker involves the client in the selection of problems to be tackled and provides assistance in their resolution, usually on a strictly time-limited basis.

Although the emphasis on specification of tasks has been developed primarily in the United States of America, it has already been found to have much relevance to social work in Britain.[5] In particular, its concentration on limited achievable goals is especially suited to work in busy departments, where the demand for services outruns resources. The setting of realistic and achievable goals can usefully be recorded in the form of an action plan, a copy of which can be given to the client after its contents have been agreed. In some cases, the plan would include action to be taken by both client and worker before they meet again for further discussion: letters to be written, doctors or solicitors to be consulted, changes to be attempted in disciplining children. The action plan would thus constitute an aide-mémoire, less fallible than memory itself and less open to misunderstanding or misinterpretation. In other cases, the goals specified would require a longer time-span: for example the finding of employment, the completion of a particular training course, the establishment of a committee or the building of an adventure playground. Such goals would have validity insofar as they were seen to be attainable by the clients concerned, but in some cases it would be preferable to break them down into constituent parts, or steps on the way, so that some short-term objectives were apparent. Finally, it must be emphasised that all goals must be subject to modification in the light of experience, changed circumstances and success or failure in achieving them.

4

Action and Evaluation

Careful assessment and realistic goal-setting jointly form the basis for the action phase of the social work process. This phase is thus concerned with work aimed to resolve the problems or difficulties which led to the involvement of the social worker in the first place. From time to time, it is necessary to review progress and in the light of this the situation may be reassessed and the goals adjusted. Eventually, the question of terminating the social worker's involvement arises and this is the appropriate point for a final evaluation of the work that has taken place. These aspects will be discussed at the end of this chapter but first it is necessary to examine the action phase in some detail.

The Action Phase

In the action phase of the social work process the emphasis is on providing the means whereby the client may be enabled to reach solutions to his problems, in the light of objectives agreed on at the outset. These means are to be found in three main sources: the social worker, the client and the social worker/client relationship. A simple view of the social work process is one where the client states his problem and the social worker provides the answer. This accords well with the medical model, wherein a patient describes his symptoms to a doctor and is then given a prescription which he usually perceives as a cure for his condition. It is also a fair description of the expectations of many of the clients of social workers, who assume that personal, family and community problems are capable of resolution by an expert in the same way as common diseases.

These assumptions about social work are sometimes, but not

often, correct. For example, it sometimes happens that social workers possess knowledge, influence and access to resources, all of which clients may lack but need. In the course of their work, social workers accumulate a great deal of specialised knowledge about social service provision, on which they are able to draw in the interests of their clients and sometimes giving an address or information about where to obtain a particular welfare benefit is all that is required to help the client. Furthermore, because of their status and authority, social workers are sometimes able to wield influence and exercise power in the interests of a client. They do this in part through 'knowing the ropes', being informed about the appropriate person to approach in the appropriate department; and in part through carefully chosen words in communication with officials who might otherwise be intractable in their attitudes towards a client. This activity, which amounts to 'working the system' is not without its moral dilemmas for social workers, particularly as success in obtaining resources for people whom they know because they are clients may result in others whom they do not know being deprived of what they need. On the other hand, many benefits are available to all, some on a discretionary basis according to need, and there can be nothing wrong with attempting to persuade other departments and officials to make available those resources to which clients are legitimately entitled.

In terms of resources, the social worker may likewise be in a position of authority and power. He may be able to open the door to residential and day care; to make arrangements for adaptations to the home of a physically handicapped person; to provide entry to a young people's activity group; or to offer typing and duplicating services to a community group. This aspect of the social worker's role is clearly a growing one as the range of provisions increases. It can be seen in the development of community care facilities provided by local authorities, particularly, but not only, for the mentally ill and retarded; in the growth of hostels, day training and community service opportunities, to which the probation and after-care service has access; and in the increasing interest in the voluntary sphere in providing resources for community groups and associations that need places in which to meet and help with publicity and recruitment.

Where a social worker possesses knowledge, influence and access to resources which are relevant to the solution of a client's difficulties, it is clearly improper to withhold them, or to make their availability conditional on a bargaining process which demands that in return the client should reveal his total life history or make amends for misdemeanours, such as by paying his debts. Social workers are sometimes forced by policies and rules to indulge in such forms of extortion, which may also be used to elucidate difficulties that are thought to underlie presenting problems. As was indicated in Chapter 3, presenting problems should always be evaluated realistically and appropriate help given where need is demonstrated. In any case, it is rare for the resources that the social worker can provide to act as solutions in themselves. They are rather the means by which the client may be enabled to reach a solution, a supplement to his own efforts, just as medicine prescribed by a doctor needs to be taken and acts as a support to the natural recovery process of the body.

Action by the social worker may range from the simple writing of a letter or making of a telephone call at one extreme to a lengthy and complex series of negotiations with a variety of agencies and departments at the other. Decisions about undertaking action on behalf of clients have to be based on the individual requirements of each case, but it is generally a good guiding principle to undertake nothing which the client is able to do for himself. The reasons for this are that doing things for other people tends to encourage dependence and to reduce their capacity to act for themselves; and conversely, that success in solving a problem tends to increase the ability to manage further difficulties as they arise. Since one of the aims of social work is to promote the capacity of individuals and groups to deal successfully with their problems, without the need to call on professional help, social workers are naturally reluctant to act in ways that are likely to undermine personal responsibility. They thus encourage clients to write their own letters and make their own telephone calls, except where they are incapable of doing so or where it appears important to both client and social worker that the communication should come from an 'official' source. The same principle operates throughout social work practice, however complex the nature of the action contemplated.

The client is thus regarded as an active contributor to the process of social work. It is in fact rare for clients to be so handicapped, physically, mentally or socially, that they possess no attributes that can be used in the resolution of their problems. It is true that in the early stages they often appear to be very limited in their capacity to help themselves, but that is generally because of despair and despondency that have accumulated over a lengthy period of time, giving the impression that they have given up all hope of reaching a solution. Once they have begun to talk about their difficulties and experienced the relief that comes from sharing them with an interested and sympathetic listener, it generally becomes apparent that they possess the capacity to begin work on their problems themselves, if only in simple ways at first. It is at this point that it is all too easy for a social worker to undermine the emergent capacity for self-help by taking action himself. It is sometimes particularly tempting to do so, because the social worker feels that he will be able to achieve results more speedily and efficiently than the client. This may well be true, but doing so may damage rather than reinforce the client's self-esteem. It is in any case more important that the client should take action in his own good time and in his own way if he is to reap permanent benefit, except in situations where there may be a danger to life, where it is quite legitimate and proper for the social worker to override the principle of self-determination. Examples of this are the compulsory admission of a person displaying serious symptoms of mental disorder to a psychiatric hospital or the removal of children from home into local authority care in situations where there is neglect or cruelty.

Decisions about action to be taken and who is to initiate it spring from the encounters that take place between social worker and client. These usually consist of regular meetings at the client's home or at the social worker's office, and sometimes at some other suitable venue, such as a café or a club. In the course of elucidating the problem and discussing possible solutions, the social worker encourages the client to trust him so that difficulties can be frankly and openly expressed. The social worker then tries to help the client to think about his difficulties and by the careful use of questions and comments, together with suggestions about how to tackle them, leads him to devise his own ideas for action. For the client, the benefit of the relationship lies in the sense of confidence and hopefulness which he gains from talking to a sympathetic person, who clearly believes that there is a solution to be found and offers positive suggestions. Relationships in social work are discussed at length in Chapters 9 and 10 of this book.

The action phase is characterised by constant reassessment of the situation and consequent modification of objectives. Each meeting between social worker and client provides an opportunity to discuss the progress being made, or the lack of it, and to share views about the next steps to be taken. New factors may arise which transform the situation and require a reformulation of objectives. The loss of a spouse through desertion or death, a change in employment, or a policy decision about evictions by the local housing department are all examples of new developments that are likely to require adjustments on the part of clients. Since it is events such as these, involving separation and deprivation that often form the main focus for the social worker's task, it is important to emphasise that although there may be a great deal of activity in the action phase, an equivalent amount of energy must also be devoted to the attitudes and feelings of clients.

Termination and Evaluation

The final phase of the social work process is concerned with termination and evaluation. In all forms of social work, there eventually comes a point at which it is no longer appropriate for the worker-client relationship to be continued and it may be helpful to examine various ways in which termination may occur before suggesting some principles to guide practice.

An examination of social work practice suggests that there are three kinds of termination: haphazard, pre-ordained and planned. Of these, it is probable that the first is the most common. This is the situation in which the client has no idea of the extent of his future involvement with the social worker, because it has never been discussed with him and he does not feel able to ask. Likewise, the social worker has probably given little thought to the question of termination and may assume that the case will continue indefinitely. From the client's point of view, the uncertainty is most unsatisfactory and he may react by terminating the relationship abruptly himself, by failing to keep appointments or being out when the social worker is expected to call at his home. Alternatively, if he still needs the help of the social worker, perhaps in order to secure certain material benefits, he takes the minimum initiative he judges to be necessary to obtain what he wants, but he is unlikely to regard the social work relationship as an opportunity to work co-operatively in the resolution of his difficulties. These are the clients who are often described in agency records as 'unco-operative' or 'unresponsive', when the probability is that the nature of the relationship with the social worker and its likely duration have never been made clear.

The social worker who gives little thought to termination is also likely to pay scant attention to planning and to the setting of objectives. This frequently gives rise to a situation in which caseloads are huge, with all clients regarded as 'active', even though three-quarters of them have not been contacted during the preceding year. If cases are terminated at all, then it is usually by means of administrative intervention on the part of a senior member of staff seeking tidiness, than on the basis of a carefully planned arrangement with the clients concerned. Even if caseloads are moderate and efforts are made to ensure that only active cases are retained, haphazard termination may still occur because of the mobility of the social work profession in terms of employment. It is not uncommon for clients to discover from a new social worker that his predecessor has left and the new worker himself may not stay long enough to become familiar, let alone trusted. It is not impossible to plan the termination of a relationship and the transfer to a new worker, but in practice this is rarely performed effectively.

Pre-ordained termination occurs in a number of social work

situations, particularly, but not exclusively, where they arise from some legal requirement. Thus probation orders have a set term, of between one and three years, and children for whom parental rights have been assumed by local authorities remain in care until the age of eighteen. Such termination dates are rarely unalterable, for a probation order may be discharged early for good conduct and there may be a change in circumstances that enables a child to go out of official care before the set age, but their very existence provides a target for the accomplishment of the action plan. Similar conditions arise in social work in hospitals, where patients can usually be expected to be discharged within certain time limits, according to the nature of their illnesses. The exact date is often unknown until shortly before discharge takes place and this can cause difficulties for hospital social workers, who find that their carefully planned work is disrupted by the sudden departure of the patient. Nevertheless, the hospital social worker usually works in the knowledge that there is to be an end to the social work process and can make plans accordingly, sometimes prolonging the opportunities for help to be given by referring the patient to an outside colleague or agency, such as an area team member of the local social services department or an appropriate voluntary organisation.

The principal advantages of pre-ordained termination are that both client and worker know in advance that there is to be an end to their relationship and that they know when that end is likely to be. This knowledge often acts as an incentive to make the best use of the time available, but the disadvantage is that this may be either insufficient or excessive. If the time is insufficient, it is sometimes possible to extend it on a voluntary basis. For example, some offenders choose to remain in touch with their probation officer after the formal completion of the order and some people who have been in local authority care as children keep in contact with the house parents who looked after them. If the time is excessive, it is sometimes possible to spread out the work by means of less frequent meetings, though this is rarely effective, since people's need for help usually arises from pressing problems which it is inappropriate to delay tackling. Alternatively, the time may be reduced, at any rate within certain conventional limits that, for example, allow the discharge of a probation order after about half of its length has expired, but not usually any earlier. Thus even if a probation officer believes that all the necessary work has been accomplished during the first two months of a probation order and can produce supporting evidence, the magistrates are likely to want to play safe and wait rather longer before considering discharge. They are also likely to be concerned about the public image of probation, thus putting the needs of society before the interests of the individual. In these circumstances, the probation officer must help the client to accept the reality of his situation and find ways of putting the relationship with him to a wider range of uses. Similarly, there is a legal requirement that children in foster homes should be visited at regular intervals, whether or not they need any help. It is easy for such visits to degenerate into a boring routine, but an imaginative social worker is able to find ways of using them to the benefit both of the child and of the foster parents concerned.

Not all social work is restricted by legal limitations in the ways illustrated above. In a great deal of his work with the sick, the elderly, the handicapped, problem families and adolescents, together with a vast range of group and community work, the social worker is free to set limits in conjunction with his clients. In all of these situations, there is the opportunity for planned intervention with a time-limit specified from the start. It is interesting that in Britain this approach seems to have developed more clearly in work with groups than in work with individuals and families. Group work obviously requires more planning, since it usually involves the provision of accommodation and equipment and the means to enable members to reach the venue. It also requires a regular time to be set aside, so that it is difficult to perform on a haphazard basis. A further point is that it is still regarded as experimental by many workers and for that reason alone merits more careful attention and planning. Finally, it is often organised on the basis of a set number of meetings, rather than being allowed to continue indefinitely, as this is felt to be more manageable, both for workers and for clients.

In the United States of America, there have been experiments involving planned intervention on a time-limited basis with individuals and families, with termination built into the process from the start. It is a feature of the task-centred work referred to in Chapter 3 and has also been reported elsewhere in the literature. One such experiment[1] compared short-term work consisting of eight sessions over a two-month period with long-term, open-ended work with a control group. It was found that the short-term clients thought they had gained more help from their contact with a social worker than the control group and that they saw the social work process in much more positive terms. No doubt the social workers engaged on the short-term programme took greater care to specify objectives and make the best use of the limited time available. Although it is not always safe to apply the findings of limited and specialised experiments on a general basis, the lesson from the research into short-term work confirms the experience of many social workers that when they share with clients the planning of the social work process, when they jointly set clear and manageable objectives and when there is a time limit towards which both parties are working, the outcome is likely to be much more satisfactory for both than it is in situations where intervention is haphazard. Finally, it is important to note that although the concept of short-term planned work is of limited relevance in the sphere of residential care, it may still be used in situations in which clients are away from their usual homes for purposes of assessment. Furthermore, in long-term care it is important to incorporate short- and medium-term objectives in the total programme planned for each resident.

Evaluation

A time limit also provides a natural opportunity for evaluation, when an attempt should be made jointly by social worker and client to measure progress made towards the objectives defined near the start of the case. Evaluation is a continuing process, prompted by every change and development in a case, but if its benefits are to be fully realised, there must be times when it is concentrated in the form of a general review. When work is taking place over a long period, it is helpful for evaluations to take place at regular intervals, perhaps quarterly or twice a year, and some social work agencies, notably the probation and after-care service, have such an arrangement built in to their system of case recording. Whether or not that happens in other agencies, it is vital that a thorough evaluation should take place prior to termination, since its result in part helps to determine whether intervention by the social worker should cease or alternatively be continued, but perhaps on the basis of a new set of objectives.

An evaluation in social work is concerned with two main areas: the client and the process. In discussing progress and developments, the social worker looks for ways in which the client has resolved his problems, changed his attitudes, gained greater satisfactions and achieved successes in personal relations and in the management of his own affairs. These findings should be related to the objectives previously agreed on so that it should be possible to measure, albeit subjectively and approximately, the extent to which these have been realised. Many of the improvements may be the result of influences outside the social work process, such as changes in family circumstances, employment, and peer group relationships, or the passing of an examination or the natural effects of ageing and maturity. Others, particularly in community work, may result from changes in local government policy or planning decisions that materially affect the lives of those with whom the social worker has been working. On the negative side, it is important to evaluate ways in which a situation may have deteriorated, to discover why this has happened and to explore possible alternative approaches that may lead to improvement.

The social worker should also attempt to evaluate the nature of his own contribution, to discover whether it has been helpful or unhelpful, relevant or irrelevant. It is a mark of a really mature and positive relationship if clients are able to speak frankly in this context, even to the extent of saying that the social worker has not helped very much, if at all. The reasons behind such feelings form a basis for discovering ways in which the social worker might modify his methods in order to be more helpful to clients in the future. If these negative comments can be matched with any positive ones, the social worker will be helped to a much greater understanding of his own work than is generally obtained from clients, who often appear indifferent to his ministrations. In general, remarkably little is know about the effectiveness of social work intervention and particularly about the reactions of clients to social workers. Some of the findings from research[2] suggest that social workers and clients tend to differ in their perceptions of what is important in the social work process, the former perhaps placing greater emphasis on the quality of relationships, the latter on receiving tangible help with problems. Although further research is needed in this area, social workers have many opportunities to involve clients in assessing the value of the help given. The development of social work as an effective process demands a firm commitment to self-evaluation from its practitioners.

5

Strategies of Social Intervention

The sequence of operations that together constitute the social work process demands a methodical approach if it is to be performed effectively. A simple definition of a method is the means of accomplishing an end and any process that is repeated continually over a period of time tends to acquire its own distinctive methodology. In part this springs from the nature of the process itself, which dictates how the various stages of the sequence may best be accomplished, but methods may also develop on a pragmatic basis from what appears to work successfully as a result of trial and error. Social work perhaps owes more to the latter than to the former in the development of its methodology, but the investigations of researchers are now beginning to redress the balance.

In some spheres of human activity, it is relatively easy to demonstrate a relationship between methods and the ends they are designed to achieve. Man now knows sufficient about the internal combustion engine to be able to build, maintain and repair it in certain standardised ways. Provided that the right materials and tools are used by a skilled mechanic, success can generally be predicted with confidence. In work concerned with human relationships, there is far less certainty, owing to the unpredictable nature of man himself. If it were possible to 'build, maintain and repair' human relationships in certain standardised ways, the task of the social worker would undoubtedly be simplified by being reduced to that of a mechanic dealing with a machine. It would hardly be in accordance with the needs of human beings, however, and it is because the nature of man is so complex that social workers strive to take account of individual differences and the right of all, within certain limits to lead their own lives in their own way. There are nevertheless certain aspects of social work practice, notably those concerned with social control and the use of authority, that come close to a mechanistic approach to human problems, and these are discussed further in Chapter 7.

For the most part there are few situations in social work in which a method can be applied for which the outcome can always be confidently predicted. That does not mean that social work has to be a random and haphazard activity but rather that it requires skills different from those of the mechanic. Just as the process of social work can be structured and planned according to certain guidelines and objectives, so the methods themselves are capable of analysis and degrees of probability can be attached to their application in specific case situations. Knowledge about methods is derived partly from experience and partly from research. On the side of experience, there is the knowledge accumulated by each individual social worker as his career progresses and he becomes increasingly aware of what seems to work satisfactorily, at any rate for him; and the knowledge that has become the generalised property of the profession and which is transmitted through education and training and through publications, of which this text is one example.

In more recent years, the findings of research have increased the areas of relative probability for the practice of social work. This applies not only to research into social work itself, such as the studies of brief and extended casework,[1] task-centred casework[2] and the reactions of clients to the service they have received from social workers,[3] but also to certain findings in other fields of study, such as sociology and psychology, both of which have been highly influential. Thus various investigations into the effects of institutional care[4] succeeded in modifying social workers' attitudes to the use of residential centres for their clients and thereby affected the methods used in offering help. Similarly, research into maternal deprivation[5] led social workers to give much higher priority to the maintenance of family relationships than to the removal of children from their homes into local authority care. One of the effects of the widespread dissemination of the findings of research is sometimes to start fashions in social work practice, with the result that, for example, all residential care is perceived as valueless on the basis of one report that criticised certain aspects of it. It is therefore vital to keep in mind the context to which research relates, to avoid inappropriate applications beyond the scope of the findings originally reported and to adopt a critical approach to new studies that question current practice. These maxims are now of increasing importance as more research is undertaken into social work methods. Provided that any findings are carefully scrutinised and assessed, such research promises to do much to extend the areas of certainty in social work practice.

As well as pointing practice in new directions, research fulfils another important function in keeping the social worker in touch with developments in methods of intervention. Although he is more than a mechanic, he still has the equivalent of machinery and tools to be kept in working order or replaced when they are no longer effective. Much of the machinery of social work was put together at a relatively early stage of its development as a profession and its practitioners sometimes appear to be reluctant to replace it, although there are clear signs that some parts of it are now outmoded. One reason for this may be that to some extent the construction of various parts of the machinery has been carried out as if by rival firms working to different designs, sometimes with the conviction that they were seeking radically different ends. These differences are reflected in the divisions within the profession, in relation to both specialist interests and preferred methods of intervention. Present-day conditions require new approaches to methods of intervention, but these must be considered in the context of social work's traditional methodology, which is discussed below.

Traditional Approaches

In the history of social work, four distinctive methodological approaches have emerged, with claims that they are different and special. These are casework, group work, community work and residential work. In spite of the differences that have been claimed for them, however, it is far from easy to define the boundaries of each with clarity, since they overlap in many ways and in recent years have perhaps moved closer together. Nevertheless they are treated separately in the discussion which follows.

Casework is usually regarded as the best established branch of social work and can trace its origins in Britain as far back as the Charity Organisation Society in London in the late nineteenth century.[6] At that time 'casework' was used simply to describe work on cases and apart from emphasising that it should be an organised and systematic process, directed towards certain ends and properly recorded, its proponents did not conceive of it as a kind of methodological creed in the way that many subsequent practitioners came to view it. In its later history, casework became primarily associated with work with individuals, with special reference to their emotional and mental functioning, albeit in the context of family and environment. Thus it has been described as a 'psychosocial therapy'[7] and a 'problem-solving process';[8] and the principles on which it is thought to be based have been expounded in terms of relationships.[9] This narrowed focus has led to major criticisms of casework as a social work method.[10] It is suggested that while the emphasis on the inner functioning of the individual in mental and emotional terms may be valid for a proportion of the clients of social workers, it is an inadequate method for dealing with the full range of problems and needs which are found in the caseloads of most general social work agencies, such as social services and probation and after-care departments. Individuals, no less than families or groups, are often grappling with difficulties that arise less from their own pathology than from the environment and the social system, both of which thereby become the legitimate concern of the social worker, but for neither of which is casework in its narrower sense an appropriate method.

In order to deal with this difficulty, some workers have abandoned the purist concept of casework and attempted to stretch its meaning to encompass a much wider range of helping activities. Carried to an extreme, this may be interpreted as an attempt at omnipotence, but even at a more moderate level, there is inevitable confusion about the precise meaning of casework and the term is consequently devalued. In this sense, it has probably become identical with the term 'social work' itself, with the unfortunate consequence of seeming to exclude from that heading work with groups and communities, unless these could somehow be distorted to conform with casework ideologies.

Such distortions are apparent in the attempts to develop subsystems of casework, most notably in the forms of marital and family casework. As each of these appeared, they must have seemed like logical extensions of casework, since the emphasis on the individual was at first strongly retained. Thus, in marital casework, the two partners were usually seen separately (or perhaps only one partner was seen), the emphasis was on helping them as individuals and only occasionally were there joint interviews, commonly towards the end of the process, as if to demonstrate tangibly that reconciliation had been achieved. Similarly, in family casework, contact with the family was at first seen as an additional means of helping the individual client and it was rare for the family as a whole to be interviewed. Parents might be seen, separately or together, but once again the purpose was to facilitate the work with the formally designated client, usually one or more of the children.

Inevitably it became apparent that there was more to marriages and families than the individuals of which they were made up and this led to an important change in focus. The 'client' now became the marriage or the family rather than the individual, more emphasis was placed on interviews in which were present both partners in the marital pair or all members of the family, adults and children alike, and the focus moved to the dynamics of the interrelationships involved. At this point, work with individuals became work with pairs and family groups and in retrospect the term 'casework' does not seem to be particularly appropriate. It was here, also, that casework overlapped with the second strand in traditional social work methodology, group work.

Group work is a fairly general term used in a number of fields to describe various forms of activity, whether in work itself or in learning or therapy, in which the principal emphasis is on the group, rather than on the individuals which constitute its membership. There is thus a great deal of group work to be found in such spheres as industry, business and education as well as in social work. In the latter field, some attempts have been made to set limits, notably in the use of the term 'social group work', but this is not defined in the same way by all social workers and so is limited as a means of clarification. It is used here to describe any group work performed by social workers.

In Britain, social group work has not been developed to anything like the extent of casework, although there is now growing interest in its application, partly as a result of dissatisfaction with the effectiveness of casework in some situations and partly because recent legislation seems to demand it. Both of these reasons apply to work with young offenders, who often appear to show little response to individual casework and for whom the intermediate treatment provisions of the Children and Young Persons Act, 1969, have been interpreted as encouraging a group work approach. As with casework, group work covers a broad spectrum. At one extreme, it is seen in pseudo-psychiatric terms in which groups are concerned with therapeutic discussion of emotional difficulties; at the other extreme are the many kinds of activity groups, in which the emphasis is on shared work and enjoyment, from which psychological and emotional benefits are expected to materialise; and in between is a wide range of group work involving various mixtures of discussion and activity. The possibility of so many different definitions of the term 'social group work' means that it has similar limitations to 'casework' in demonstrating clearly the nature of the social worker's activities.

Like social group work, *community work* also presents a number of difficulties when attempts are made to define it as a social work method. It attracts interest well outside the boundaries of social work, notably from educators, planners, voluntary organisations, self-help groups, churches and politicians. As with social group work and casework, community work is also a portmanteau term covering a number of different, albeit overlapping, methods of working. In its more traditional form, it has been known as community organisation, in which the emphasis is generally placed on co-operation and co-ordination between statutory and voluntary bodies engaged in social welfare. A second strand is community development, pioneered in new and under-developed countries, with an emphasis on enabling people to cope with the problems of rapid technological and social change, including industrialisation and urbanisation. More recently, this approach has been transferred to developed countries, such as Britain and the United States, to focus on the problems of communities in new towns and declining inner city areas. A third strand is community action, where the emphasis is on enabling community groups to form and through united strength to gain benefits, obtain redress for injustices or fight proposals that appear detrimental to their daily lives. Community action raises the possibility of strategies that are orientated to conflict as well as to consensus and negotiation. All three aspects of community work contain elements that are relevant to the practice of social work, but they are too easily confused and misunderstood when discussed together in a general way. Such discussion may also give the appearance that social work seeks to extend its boundaries by incorporating the whole of community work exclusively, when the reality is that only certain aspects may be appropriate to the social worker's methodology.

A further problem about community work is the difficulty of finding satisfactory definitions of the term 'community' itself. Thus it is sometimes used in a geographical sense (for example, a housing estate), sometimes in terms of an interest (for example, a recreational or religious interest group) and sometimes when referring to a need group (for example, the elderly or the blind). Even if it can be satisfactorily defined in a specific situation, how does a social worker actually work with a community? Unless all its members reside in the same place or belong to the same organisation, it is difficult to conceive of work with a community as such. Rather does the social worker deal with the individuals and groups which make up the community with which he is concerned. The community then becomes the setting or context within which he operates, using whichever aspects of social work methodology are appropriate.

The same argument applies with even greater force to *residential work*. The care of people living in a residential centre is clearly a task that requires a range of abilities and skills, including domestic service, catering, building construction and maintenance, the management of stock and the keeping of accounts, as well as personal attention to both physical and emotional needs. Although it may be tempting to regard all of these as aspects of social work, particularly in the case of small residential centres such as family group children's homes, to do so both distorts the concept of social work as a distinctive activity and devalues the contribution made by others with specialist expertise, such as nurses, caterers and accountants. It is thus appropriate to see residential work not as a method, but as a setting in which social work may be practised in conjunction with the work of other professionals. Furthermore, as in community work, the social worker in a residential centre is involved both with individuals and with groups.

The argument so far, then, is that the familiar division of social work into four methods is no longer an adequate model as a basis for practice. Furthermore, it is suggested that it is inappropriate to regard them as methods at all, since they each incorporate a wide range of activities and overlap at various points, thus ceasing to be distinctive. Their value lies in the fact that, combined together, they contain the total range of social work methods, which must now be redefined in different terminology. Before that is done, however, there are three common features to be postulated which between them provide the framework for social work practice. These are: context, focus and dimension.

A Framework for Practice

Human beings do not exist in limbo but in a variety of social situations and it is these that provide the *context* for social work practice. These situations include individual isolation, pairs (as in the marital relationship), families, a whole variety of group formations, the range of communities already mentioned and institutional living, whether small or large scale. Few people exist exclusively in only one of these contexts, so that in the early stages of a case it may not be clear which is the most important or whether there is more than one involved. The relative importance of different contexts should become clear as the assessment phase of the social work process progresses. In some cases, the context may alter, as the circumstances of the client change, as, for example, when an elderly person moves from living alone into a residential centre. In other cases, there may be two or more distinctive contexts relevant to one case, as happens when a child is in a children's home and the social worker is concerned with him and also with his parents and family from whom he is parted. What is vitally important is that the social worker should be clear about the context of the problems with which he is working; and that where there is more than one in a particular case, he should assess the relative importance of each and the relationships between them, as the basis for deciding where to concentrate his efforts. If he fails to do this, he may become confused about his objectives and that will lead to inappropriate work and wasted time and energy, as well as mystifying the clients concerned.

Most social workers have to work in more than one context in the course of a day and perhaps the residential worker provides the most obvious example of this, since the very nature of his task requires the ability to switch attention quickly from one situation to another. Thus in the space of little more than an hour, the warden of an old people's home may provide individual help to a resident, pacify an argumentative husband and wife, take the chair at a residents' committee and speak with members of a local community group concerned with the welfare of the elderly. As the concept of the field social worker's task is enlarged, he too is increasingly expected to make rapid switches from one context to another, but for all workers this should be made easier by the recognition that the methods in each context are basically the same.

There is one reservation that needs to be mentioned here, which is that working in more than one context may at times be impossible because of the conflict thereby engendered. This is particularly likely to happen in the community context, where meeting the short-term needs of individuals and families may appear to delay the satisfaction of longer-term needs in the total community. For example, a social worker pressing the local council for special adaptations to the homes of physically handicapped people may be seen as prejudicing the outcome of a general campaign by tenants to gain improvements for all. Discussion with those involved may produce an acceptable compromise or alternatively, teamwork, in which individuals specialise in working in distinctive contexts, can provide a different means of resolution, but the involvement of social workers with community groups seeking united action at the same time as their colleagues are undertaking what may be seen as counter-productive work in individual or family contexts poses problems which the profession has yet to resolve.

Whatever the context, it is essential for social workers to have a clearly defined *focus* for their intervention. There appear to be three related elements in the focus of social work, often described in terms of the person, the problem and the situation. The client is obviously the centre of attention in social work, but to understand what this means it is necessary to be able to distinguish him from other human beings who face problems in their own particular situations, but resolve them without professional assistance. How does the client differ from others in society? The answer to this question has usually been given in terms of differences between individuals in their ability to cope with life's stresses and social work has then been regarded as helping those unable to help themselves. This goes some way towards clarifying the focus, but it does not narrow it down sufficiently to distinguish it from the work of many others who can legitimately claim to 'help those unable to help themselves', for example doctors and the staff of the Supplementary Benefits Commission. It also ignores the reality that most people are able to deal with their own problems if suitably guided and encouraged, which is the form that much social work takes.

An alternative definition for the focus of social work might be found in the nature of the problems dealt with by social workers. The responsibilities of most social workers are defined for them by a mixture of law, policy, precedent and practice and it is not difficult to produce a comprehensive list of their duties in any particular agency. Even so, this does not provide a clear definition of focus. Social workers deal with such problems as physical handicap and juvenile delinquency, but they do not do so exclusively, nor does a detailed description of their responsibilities and powers clarify the exact nature of their concern. As for the third element contained in focus, that of the client's situation, this has already been redefined as the context of social work. What is needed is a term that links the client, his problem and his situation in a way that shows clearly the exact nature of the focus of social work. One such is to be found in the use of the term 'social functioning' which has emerged in the literature in recent years. Its meaning has been explored extensively by a number of writers, including Bartlett,[11] who regards it as 'a concept broad enough to encompass the profession's scope and yet clear enough to provide a focus that will stimulate integrated thinking and effort. It is a positive way of limiting the professional area of interest without having to set outer boundaries and is a way of defining what social work is that is sufficiently open ended to allow for further development'.

Bartlett views social functioning as 'coping behaviour in relation to life tasks and environmental demands'[12] and this is clearly a most useful concept for social work practice in any of the contexts set out above. Social work thus concentrates partly on supporting and reinforcing coping behaviour, partly on enabling clients to understand and master life tasks and partly on the reduction or modification of environmental demands. The emphasis given to each of these aspects obviously varies in each case, according to the needs and wishes of the client and also in relation to the extent to which changes are deemed to be possible and desirable in any or all of the three areas of focus.

The context of social work is largely defined by the client's situation and the way in which he presents himself for help. The focus springs from the nature of his problems and the role of the social worker in dealing with them in their particular context, thus creating a concern with social functioning. The final element in the framework for practice is that of *dimension*. Although this arises in part from the context and focus, it is also related to the ways in which the social worker intervenes in a given situation. The choice here lies between working with individuals, with pairs, with families and with groups, on one hand: and with working in the environment more generally on the other. None of these dimensions need be exclusive and they frequently overlap, so social workers need to be skilled at switching from one dimension to another. In many situations, it is desirable to make a choice about which dimension to use in preference to others. For example, in dealing with young offenders, there may be a choice between individual and group work. As many people who work with groups consider that their effectiveness is diminished if individual work is carried out in parallel, it may be necessary to make a clear choice between one or the other, depending on individual circumstances and the wishes of clients. (It should also be noted that some social workers prefer to mix individual and group work, having found that it can be done successfully: in such circumstances a firm decision to work in two dimensions is indicated.) Family problems provide the opportunity to work in at least three different dimensions—individual, the marital pair and the family as a whole—but it may be preferable to avoid mixing all three concurrently if the results are not to be dissipated to little effect. Community work is particularly concerned with the environmental dimension but also involves intervention with individuals and groups.

In any situation, it may be appropriate to change the dimension over the course of time, as, for example, in moving from individual to group work and back. Sometimes, however, it is not possible to work in the preferred dimension because of practical difficulties or the wishes of the client. In the former category come those circumstances where clients are away in distant residential centres, where there may not be much opportunity for contact and efforts must be concentrated on the family instead. In the second group are those who seek help with problems that involve others, but do not want them to be approached directly, although the social worker believes that this would be more helpful and effective. For this reason, marital and family problems must sometimes be dealt with in the individual dimension.

Strategies of Intervention

Context, focus and dimension provide the framework for the application of social work methods and as these are no longer to be described in familiar terms as casework, group work, community work and residential work, it is necessary to find some alternative terminology. Any term used must fulfil a number of important requirements. It must be comprehensive, in that it incorporates all of the methods used by social workers. It must be comprehensible, in that it can be clearly understood to relate to methods within the totality represented by the term 'social work', as distinct from any that may lie outside it. Finally, it must be capable of being broken down into its component parts for analysis and application in practice.

Bartlett provides one possible solution in the term 'interventive repertoire', which she conceives of as including 'multiple interventive measures and techniques, in fact, all that social work is using at any one time'.[13] She does not restrict it to direct work with clients but sees it as having very broad general application: 'Viewed this way, social work's interventive measures range from helping service given an individual by one social worker to the widest efforts to influence change in social conditions affecting large population groups'.[14] The emphasis on the idea of intervention is particularly important, since this is exactly what the social worker is engaged in doing and this was stated at the start of this book in the first sentence of Chapter 1. The purpose of the intervention is to seek solutions to problem situations in co-operation with those involved, a concept for which Bartlett's term 'repertoire' seems inadequate, as its theatrical overtones imply the performance of a stock of set pieces in front of a passive audience. It is the dynamic nature of social work which needs to be emphasised and this seems best exemplified in the term 'strategies of social intervention'.[15] 'Strategy' in its original military sense means the art of conducting a campaign and although it is now used more generally in the sense of finesse, both definitions may aptly be applied to social work intervention. A strategy in military terms also implies engagement with the other side and once again this can be translated into social work terms to stress the dynamic nature of intervention, in which both social worker and client are involved together, though as partners, in a war against whatever difficulties or problems constitute the 'enemy'.

Strategies of social intervention may thus be seen as made up of a range of different and distinctive activities applied in a variety of combinations in the process of social work, with the purpose of fulfilling objectives related to social functioning. The strategies are available to all social workers, though in practice they are used differentially and with different emphases, according to the nature of the task in hand as elicited by the social assessment. The criteria for selecting any strategy should be its appropriateness in relation to the needs of the client and the likelihood of its achieving the objectives in the case. In this text, strategies are for convenience divided into those concerned with interpersonal relationships and those relevant to intervention in the environment.

In many ways, there is little that is new about this formulation of social work methodology, since it reflects what social workers themselves have long been accustomed to doing, though often intuitively rather than consciously. It is also a form of systems theory, an increasingly significant conceptual approach to social work, in which the different elements involved in the social work process are analysed as interacting systems.[16] For the present text, the systems have deliberately been described in terms of context, focus and dimension, because these provide a clear analytical framework for social work practice in Britain. With this as a basis, social workers should be in possession of a more flexible and wide-ranging model than in the past and thereby be freed from rigid allegiances to specific and narrowly defined ideologies of intervention. They should also be able to conceptualise with greater clarity about the nature of their work.

Strategies and tactics are often associated together and the latter are usually defined as the art of manœuvring in the face of the enemy. There are clearly some situations in which the social worker may feel this definition to be apt, particularly when faced with hostility from officials in other departments, who seem unprepared to accept his pleadings on behalf of needy clients. In the more general sense of purposeful procedure, tactics represent the 'skill' aspects of social work, discussed in detail in Chapters 9 to 12. The next three chapters are devoted to a detailed analysis of strategies of social intervention, and as a convenient means of reference, the points made in this chapter are summarised in the table that appears below. As has already been emphasised, the categories are not mutually exclusive, since it is often necessary to combine them in various ways and move rapidly from one to another. To achieve good standards of practice, however, social workers may find it helpful to clarify in their own minds the context, focus and dimension applicable to each new case before deciding on appropriate strategies of intervention.

TABLE I: A FRAMEWORK FOR SOCIAL INTERVENTION

Context (Situational definition)	*Focus* (Social functioning)	*Dimension* (Social work approach)	*Strategies of Social Intervention* (Social work methodology)
Isolation	Coping behaviour	Individual	Interpersonal intervention
Pair	Life tasks	Pair	Environmental intervention
Family	Environmental demands	Family	
Group		Group	
Community		Environment	
Residential centre			

6

Interpersonal Intervention

(i) *Providing and Enabling*

The strategies presented in this chapter and the two that follow it are divided for convenience into two groups: those involving interpersonal intervention, largely but not exclusively with clients (Chapters 6 and 7), and those used in environmental intervention or work on behalf of clients. The strategies discussed are those which appear to be in widespread use, but it is recognised that there may be others of a more specialised nature, which are less commonly known or applied. Furthermore, although the various strategies are here separated for purposes of discussion, in practice they overlap and become inter-related, and it is usually necessary to use a carefully planned permutation of strategies in each case.

With these qualifications in mind, it is possible to divide the strategies used in interpersonal intervention into four separate categories, in each of which there are subdivisions. The four categories are: providing, enabling, influencing and creating, terms which have the virtue of simplicity and make it easier to grasp exactly what is involved in the practice of social work. In the past, not all of these terms have been readily accepted as appropriate descriptions of what social workers do and there has been a tendency to place exaggerated emphasis on the enabling aspects of the task at the expense of the others. In this discussion, they are presented on an equal basis in the belief that their value is not simply intrinsic, but lies in their appropriateness for a given situation. Providing and enabling are discussed in this chapter; influencing and creating are dealt with in Chapter 7.

Providing

When Wootton[1] proposed that social workers should abandon some of their more ambitious aims and concentrate on acting as private secretaries to the poor, it was hardly surprising that she provoked a reaction of considerable indignation among members of the profession. Her attack was interpreted as an attempt to devalue much of the fundamental work in repairing human relationships in which social workers had come to regard themselves as experts, but the representation of this in the literature had become so distorted and exaggerated that it is understandable that Wootton was misled into believing that what she criticised could be taken as the reality of the situation. That seems most unlikely, since social workers in general have never been concerned exclusively with what might be called 'relationship therapy'. In Britain especially, their responsibilities have always involved them in many other tasks including the provision of material aid and practical assistance. They have sometimes regretted the necessity for these latter aspects of their work and attempted to minimise their importance, but as the defects of national welfare provision have become more apparent in recent years and the results of economic and social change have been seen as aggravating the consequences of poverty and deprivation, the need for renewed concentration on practical issues has become unavoidable. Providing strategies may now be seen to include information and advice, material aid and education.

Information and Advice. Many people seeking help from a social worker are found to be in need of information about statutory or voluntary services, both to enable them to obtain their rights and also to assist them in making full use of social provisions that are appropriate to their needs. Although there are specialist agencies in some places, such as citizens' advice bureaux or family advice centres, which cater for this type of problem, many towns and villages are without such facilities and this means that social workers are often faced with requests for information about social resources. Furthermore, such requests frequently arise in cases in which they are involved for other reasons. It is important, therefore that social workers should have a full working knowledge of welfare services and resources and that the knowledge should be up-to-date and accurate. If each worker does not possess it himself, he should know where to obtain it and be prepared to get it for the client. As welfare legislation is now so complicated, it is arguable that all social work departments should appoint specialists who would concentrate on keeping up-to-date with legislation and changes in rules, and be available to supply appropriate information at the request of social workers. It is also important that social workers should not neglect the specialist knowledge available in other departments and agencies, such as the Supplementary Benefits Commission, the Department of Employment, local authority departments and the many voluntary organisations concerned with social welfare. These aspects are discussed further in Chapter 8.

It is often necessary to engage in discussion with the client in order to establish clearly the exact nature of the information required. This sometimes leads to a fuller consideration of family problems and the use of alternative strategies, but these should not be inflicted on clients as the price to be paid for the information needed. That this has sometimes happened is demonstrated in the research of Mayer and Timms,[2] who found that some clients seeking practical help had felt themselves forced into disclosing intimate personal matters which seemed to them irrelevant to what they wanted, which they felt they did not in any case get.

The information discussed so far has been that of a mainly factual nature designed to increase knowledge about the availability of services. There is another kind of information in the possession of social workers which can be equally valuable to the client. This is information about how to set about achieving an objective and much of it is built up from local knowledge and experience, which makes social workers who stay in the same district for many years a particularly valuable resource to their clients and colleagues. Such knowledge may simply be the name of the person in another department or organisation who is likely to be of most assistance in a particular situation. At a more complex level, it may be the kind of knowledge required by a community group about how to proceed in a campaign, the most appropriate order in which to make approaches to other bodies. Some of this knowledge also springs from the social worker's previous experience with other clients, which, used selectively and keeping in mind what is appropriate, may be of assistance to individuals and groups in setting objectives, ordering priorities and planning programmes.

Information of this kind, providing answers to the question of how to get things done, often overlaps with the giving of advice. Social workers have tended to view advice with suspicion, believing, often rightly, that people accept and follow only that advice which accords with what they wish to do in any case. Another criticism of advice is that if people decide to act on it and the outcome is unsuccessful, the social worker will be blamed for causing the resultant difficulties and his credibility will thereby be devalued. These are important reservations about the use of advice and it is certainly wise for social workers to be cautious in dispensing it. There are some circumstances, however, in which the social worker's greater knowledge of a situation may suggest that he should make it available in the form of advice to an individual or group contemplating a particular course of action. Thus he may advise a community group to communicate with a councillor whom he has good reason to believe will be receptive to their requests, rather than another one they contemplate approaching, whom he thinks would be less sympathetic. In the case of an individual, he may advise a particular approach, perhaps of apology or contrition, towards a spouse or parent, as a means of resolving a relationship problem, or a change in methods of disciplining a child as a means of improving behaviour. Where appropriate, therefore, the social worker should not hesitate to make available to his clients the information and advice he possesses and which he has reason to believe may be to their benefit. If he is able to indicate that they are free to act otherwise if they wish and also that his views are not infallible, the disadvantages of advice giving should be minimised.

Material Aid. Although the provisions of social legislation, notably those relating to welfare benefits, have done much to reduce the social worker's concern with material aid, which was one of the main considerations in the early days of the development of social work in the late nineteenth century, the continuance of gaps in the welfare state makes it necessary for social workers to retain a concern in this area. The need for such assistance as a preventive measure was recognised in statute in the Children and Young Persons Act, 1963, which enables local authorities to provide help in kind and, exceptionally, in cash to prevent the need for children to be received into care. This Act followed fifteen years of experience in preventive work by the staff of children's departments, during which it became clear that material aid could often be a valuable measure in restoring equilibrium in a family without its first being broken up.

Material aid may be provided in three ways. The first is direct financial help through a grant for a specific purpose. In work with families this may be money to enable them to buy clothing or furniture at a time when no other source of funds is available. In the case of offenders released from institutional sentences, money may be provided through the probation and after-care service to enable them to buy tools and equipment that will assist them in resuming their normal occupation. It is also possible in some agencies, such as probation and after-care, to make modest loans to clients for specific purposes.

The second form of material aid is indirect financial assistance. This is most clearly demonstrated in the use of rent guarantees in local authority social service work, where eviction of a family is prevented by means of a financial arrangement between the department and the housing authority, not always with the knowledge of clients. It is also seen in instances where a department pays for the cost of holidays for the physically handicapped, the mentally retarded or the elderly; or pays a contribution towards the rent or running costs of accommodation used for meetings of community groups, for example an old people's club, playgroup or residents' association.

The third type of material aid is provision in kind, which often takes the form of clothing and equipment. Many social work agencies have a store of furniture, bedding, clothing, prams, cookers, toys and so on, which they are prepared to make available to needy clients, either free of charge or for a small sum in return. In a very different sense, but still under the heading of material aid, some agencies provide support to community groups and organisations by offering typing and duplicating services and accommodation for meetings free of charge.

It seems appropriate to mention here that clients often approach social workers for material aid which they are unable to provide, either because the law does not permit it or because the necessary resources are not available. In these circumstances, it is important to indicate this to the client, as soon as it has become clear that the client requires help that is not available, rather than making it an opportunity to look for other ways of intervening, which is sometimes but not always appropriate. Clients may then be referred elsewhere or an attempt may be made to 'bend' agency rules on the grounds that it is a special case. In some circumstances, it is necessary to indicate to the client that there do not appear to be any ways in which his need for material aid can be met, other than through his own efforts. Social workers, who like to see themselves in a positive helping role, find this aspect of their work uncomfortable, but it is important to be realistic and not create in clients false expectations which are incapable of fulfilment. It may also be possible to assist them in reorganising the management of their resources in ways that will provide some easement of their difficulties.

Material aid is a tangible demonstration of the giving and receiving elements in social work, which are perhaps less obviously present in other strategies. The ability to give and to withhold confers power on social workers and it is vital for them to use it responsibly in the interests of clients and not in the satisfaction of any particular dogma to which they may subscribe, for example a belief that money solves all problems. It is also not sufficiently recognised that there are giving aspects to the role of client, which can be influential in helping them to heal psychological wounds and restore self-esteem. At its simplest level, the provision of a cup of tea and its acceptance by the social worker may be sufficient to enable the client to feel that he is not entirely helpless and worthless. Other clients may choose to give token presents at Christmas or at the ending of their contact with the social worker, while others may wish to contribute articles to the agency's store of clothing and equipment, from which they may themselves have benefited in less favourable times. Finally, the careful use of material aid can be the first step in the development of a helping relationship with an individual or family, demonstrating the care and concern of the social worker and indicating that he is able to provide relevant help to those in need. In work with so-called 'problem' families, in which apathy and helplessness are sometimes the predominant features, material aid can be a means of beginning to restore self-esteem and the capacity for members to become active again in helping themselves.

Education. Although education itself is the concern of professionals other than social workers, there are many educational aspects in social work practice. Some of these are concerned with learning how to live, to deal effectively with life's tasks and to plan for the future, where these are appropriate to the needs of the client. In discussing these issues with clients the social worker can contribute from his own experience and that of others and thereby increase knowledge about the range of opportunities and choices available. Other aspects of education in social work intervention are concerned with practical problems, the resolution of which leads to improved satisfactions in life. Handicapped people may be helped to learn practical tasks that increase their range of activities; educationally retarded people may be taught to read and write; groups of young people may be helped to learn how to plan and carry out their own activities. Sometimes it is necessary to help young children to learn how to play and then find ways of helping parents to carry forward the process demonstrated to them by the social worker. Other parents may need basic instruction in household skills such as cookery or redecoration. As a final example, social workers intervening in the community context are often concerned with helping local groups, such as tenants' associations, to conduct their business efficiently and effectively. This involves learning about the creation of suitable organisational structures, the election of officers and committees, the conduct of meetings and the management of financial resources.

Educational opportunities sometimes arise because social worker and client share a common interest, about which they can learn together. This is particularly appropriate in work with clients with whom contact is compulsory, but who appear to have no particular problems to be resolved. Thus probation officers are sometimes able to make supervision of offenders effective and beneficial through a shared interest such as a sport or a hobby, which then becomes the basis for any relationship that develops between them. In these situations the roles of teacher and learner may well be exchanged, enabling the client to display competence in an area of knowledge or expertise and to transmit some of it to the social worker. This can be of great importance to young people in helping them to develop self-confidence, as well as providing them with a safe means of relating to adult figures. The social worker benefits as well in terms of increased specialist knowledge, together with understanding about human nature. Most social workers acknowledge readily the enormous extent to which they learn from their clients and see this as one of the privileges of their role.

To ensure that effective educational help is given, the social worker may need to call on other specialists, such as domestic science teachers, accountants or youth leaders to provide the necessary skills. Unless the social worker is himself an expert in a particular field, it is more appropriate to use outside specialists, but he retains an educational role in assisting clients to make full use of the resources available to them, such as classes, clubs and other learning opportunities available in the community. Although little has been written in recent years about the educational role of the social worker, it is not a new idea. One of the texts used for many years in the training of probation officers was called 'Probation and Re-education',[3] but now that this has fallen out of fashion it seems important to place renewed emphasis on the educational function of the social worker. Moreover, it could be said to be even more important now as a means of assisting clients to cope with the complexities of life and to learn new sources of satisfaction in rapidly changing social conditions.[4]

Enabling

Before a social worker provides a practical solution to a client's problem, it may be necessary to do some groundwork. The purpose of this is either to enable the client to reveal the full complexity of his problems so that the most appropriate solution may be provided, or to help him make use of the solution itself in a more effective way. In other situations, there may be no practical solution available or it may emerge that the request for material aid is a presenting problem underlying which there are other, more fundamental difficulties with which he wishes to be helped. Enabling activities are based on the assumption that through the process of a conversation or discussion carefully guided by the social worker, clients become better able to manage their own lives and the problems which are afflicting them. This assumption applies as much to groups as to individuals, as is shown in the following discussion of different aspects of enabling.

Release of Feelings. People and groups facing problems have a tendency to become emotionally stimulated, with their feelings very near the surface and often much more openly expressed than is their usual habit. It is in these situations that contact with a social worker often occurs and it is therefore a common characteristic of clients, whether singly or in groups, that they are anxious to ventilate their feelings in the presence of a sympathetic listener. When strong feelings are obviously present but not being openly expressed and experience suggests that it would be beneficial for them to be released, the social worker takes steps to do so. This is done by conveying to the client that feelings may be expressed safely and also by tentative suggestions as to the possible nature of the emotions involved. It may also be done in a more directly interpretative manner by 'playing back' to the client how he appears to the social worker to be feeling.

The rationale for allowing and encouraging the expression of feelings is the knowledge that it often has therapeutic value for the client. 'Getting it off one's chest' is an everyday expression that recognises the value of emotional release. It enables people to sort out confused feelings, to give expression to largely negative emotions, such as fear, anxiety, hostility and aggression and in general to share with someone else the burden of coping with life's problems. For many people the opportunities to obtain this kind of release are limited and even non-existent, since there are often emotional obstacles to the sharing of such intimate and disturbing feelings with close relatives or neighbours, who themselves may in any case be implicated in the situation or may be regarded as unreceptive. Members of families and groups often experience alarming feelings about each other which they are afraid to express in case of a hostile response, yet it may be important for these emotions to be revealed and discussed if their difficulties are to be resolved.

In all of these circumstances, an outsider who is not himself emotionally involved in the conflicts may act as a catalyst who enables feelings to be expressed in a safe way, without fear of mutual self-destruction. A common example of this is the client who seeks help with an emotionally tense situation, perhaps a marital difficulty. Such clients often talk almost without stopping for an hour or more, during which long suppressed negative feelings are expressed with very little need for active intervention by the social worker, who merely asks an occasional question or gives encouragement to continue. At the end of the interview, the client is profuse in gratitude, claims to feel much better and departs with an invitation to return for further discussion, which is rarely kept. Although this cannot be used to prove the value of emotional release in solving problems, since the eventual outcome is often unknown to the social worker, the client's attitude at the end of the interview suggests that, at least temporarily, the opportunity to express feelings freely has been of some positive benefit. Failure to return may also mean that such emotional release has enabled the client to find new ways of coping with difficulties by reducing anxiety and the feeling of isolation.

The element of making it safe to express feelings is particularly important in groups, in which strong tensions may develop covertly that affect the life and work of the group, without the cause being explicit. Here the social worker must be able to detect what is wrong and help members to express feelings and thus bring the tensions out into the open, where they can be discussed rationally. Many groups founder because of a denial of the existence of conflict, either about objectives or about the methods of achieving them; or because of interpersonal tensions that are apparent but have not been openly acknowledged. Conflict of feelings is rarely easy to deal with and this may lead social workers to avoid difficult issues or hold back from intervening when opportunities to bring them out into the open occur. Yet the expression of conflict is often the first step in the process of finding a constructive and rational solution. It is important for social workers to accept that conflict and difference of opinion are characteristic of many of the situations with which they deal and to learn to direct their expression towards constructive ends, rather than colluding with clients in denying their reality.

Emotional release is not always a suitable strategy in socia work. There are some people for whom expression of feelings is in itself so traumatic that the consequences tend to be worse than if the emotions remain contained. These are people who suffer from excessive guilt about their negative emotions, the release of which may propel them into serious depression necessitating medical care. Although such people are not easily identified, as they may well appear at first sight to have good control of their emotions, it is a sound general principle to limit the expression of feelings in any one interview or meeting, if necessary cutting it short in a sensitive way. It is also helpful to warn clients that they may subsequently experience feelings of guilt and remorse about what they have revealed to the social worker, but that these are natural after-effects which will pass away after reflection. Another group of clients for whom expression of feelings is usually not appropriate consists of those who have become habitual releasers and tell their story to whoever is willing to listen. Although they obviously derive considerable satisfaction from opportunities to talk about themselves, it is usually found that the release of feelings makes little difference to their subsequent behaviour or to their ability to cope with life. With such people, alternative strategies are usually required, such as those that involve influencing the client. As a general principle, it is usually suggested that the expression of feelings should always be purposeful, that is directed towards particular objectives related to the restoration or enhancement of the client's social functioning.

Clarification. Confused emotional states are often accompanied by dislocated thought processes, adding to the stress experienced by the client. Thus, parallel to the strategy of releasing feelings is one which enables clients to re-order their thinking about their situation and this is known as clarification. In some cases, as with release of feelings, it may be sufficient for the client to have an opportunity to talk to a sympathetic listener, during the process of which clarification takes place through verbal expression and the making of previously unperceived links between different aspects of the problem. There are many people whose understanding of a problem is enhanced by hearing themselves speak about it to someone else.

In other circumstances, there may be a need for extensive discussion, possibly over a period of time, before the client is able to think clearly about his situation. This kind of discussion is particularly important where decisions of great significance to the client are involved, such as leaving home or a marital partner, choice or change of career or early retirement. The rationale for allowing plenty of time is that the most appropriate decisions in life are usually based on careful consideration of alternative possibilities, a process that involves thought rather than emotion if it is to be successfully accomplished. In many cases, however, the clients of social workers are swayed more by emotion than by intellect and it is this very factor that often propels them into difficulties that lead to referral. The social worker can help here by encouraging a rational approach to problem-solving, in the hope that the decisions that emerge will produce better results for the client than in the past. This point of view is sometimes criticised because it seems to involve imposing the mode of behaviour of the social worker for whom rationality is essential on clients to whom it is often alien. Although it is necessary for social workers to accept that life styles different from their own may be necessary and effective for others, it is important that they should also recognise any capacity for clear thinking, whether manifest or latent, that the client possesses, and use it where appropriate as an aid to the solution of problems.

The use of clarification is particularly important in working with groups and especially with those community associations that are seeking to achieve changes in the circumstances of their members but have difficulty in charting a suitable course. Here the social worker's role is to help the group to clarify the issues and to study their ramifications, and also to select short-term and long-term objectives, putting the desired courses of action into an order of priority. This is also relevant to work with individuals and families and in all situations there is one pitfall to be avoided. In trying to understand the circumstances of the client or the group, a social worker inevitably draws certain conclusions about what is happening and what would be the best course of action in his own view. It can be tempting to impose this view of the situation on the people concerned, rather than trying to remain an unbiased observer who is attempting to help others decide for themselves what is the best course to take. The social worker should not refrain from helping people to consider the likely consequences of any decisions they may take, particularly any which he thinks may lead to an undesirable outcome for them, but he is rarely in a position to take away from them the power to act as they wish. The only exceptions are situations in which the social worker is in a position of authority and control over the lives of clients, discussed in Chapter 7, and other situations in which the wishes of clients are totally at variance with the role of the social worker, and he is forced to withdraw, as when a group of young people with whom he is working decides to go on a shoplifting expedition. Even in such extreme circumstances, it is unlikely that the social worker would withdraw before he had made numerous attempts to clarify the situation for the group and also used any appropriate influencing strategies, as alternative measures.

Encouragement. Although release of feelings and clarification are sometimes sufficient to enable the client to resume full responsibility for managing his life, this is not always the case and it thus becomes necessary to find ways of stimulating self-help. This aspect of enabling is often called 'support', a term widely used in the social work literature. Its weakness, as many including Hollis[5] have pointed out, is that it is a very general term, which can aptly be applied to a great deal of social work intervention, including release of feelings and clarification. Perhaps its main value is the emphasis it places on building up the strengths of the client while trying to minimise the influence of any weaknesses, but for the sake of clarity it seems preferable to use a more specific term, such as 'encouragement'.

Encouragement means to put courage in, to inspire with hope and also to cherish. For many people, encouragement is something taken for granted, on which they rely at home, at work and in their leisure activities. For social workers, it is a fundamental form of support from colleagues and superiors which they need for the effective performance of their work. On a much larger scale, most of the greatest individual and collective human achievements owe debts to the encouragement received from others. One of the significant characteristics of encouragement is that it appears to be most effective in the context of warm and trusting relationships, which is why so much emphasis is placed on this particular aspect of social work intervention.

Clients are frequently people who are either almost totally deprived of encouragement in their daily lives and therefore without hope; or the encouragement they receive is not appropriate to the resolution of the life tasks with which they are struggling. It is therefore sensible and relevant for social workers to attempt to make good this deficiency. There are three aspects to this, all implied in the definitions of encouragement given above.

First, for encouragement to have any meaning and effect at all, it is necessary for the social worker to have a genuine care and concern for other people. This is what is meant by cherishing, so although encouragement can be defined as a psychological technique to be applied when appropriate, it is not something that can be switched on and off mechanically, since it stems from the total personality and outlook of the worker and has to be applied in the context of a relationship with the client. Anyone who is not concerned for the wellbeing of others, or who does not believe in the value of what he is doing, is unlikely to be able to offer much in the way of encouragement to others. The caring and cherishing approach of a social worker can help to restore self-esteem and confidence in those who are emotionally starved or who have long experience of rejecting relationships.

The second aspect of encouragement is that it helps people to feel better about themselves and provides them with hope where none may have existed before. To a client, it is encouraging to find both that his problems are not unique but have been experienced by others before him and also that there is some real prospect of a solution being found, if he and the social worker grapple together with the difficulties. The social worker's confidence and belief in the possibility of improvement may also act as a source of inspiration to the client that enables him to begin taking action for himself. A situation can be transformed when a social worker conveys to an individual or a group that not only are there possible ways out of an impasse, but that with his encouragement the clients concerned can act to solve the problems themselves. It does not necessarily matter if at first the client acts more to please the social worker than because he genuinely believes that change can occur, since the one often produces the other. Furthermore, just as in ordinary life experience, inspiration sometimes encourages a person to venture beyond what he has previously assumed to be his limitations to discover fresh abilities that further enhance his capacity for problem solving and achieving personal satisfaction. In many community work projects, there have been individual achievements of this kind, whether or not the objectives of a group as a whole have been realised, and the people concerned have gone on to develop different interests and tackle new problems with the strength and vigour gained from encouragement in the original work.[6]

Encouragement is thus an aspect of enabling that through success tends to have a 'snowball' effect and it is part of the task of the social worker to promote this. The only qualifications that must be mentioned are that the use of encouragement needs to be related to the capacity of the client to take advantage of it, which can be discovered through trial and error in practice, and that it must be based on a realistic assessment of what is achievable or else there will be disappointment and failure for both client and worker. It is clearly useless and potentially harmful if clients are encouraged to attempt solutions or changes that are not within their capacity or potential for development. In this context, the third aspect of encouragement becomes relevant. This is reassurance, a technique which is widely practised both by professionals and by members of the public generally. Many of the realities of life are too uncomfortable or painful for people to accept, so they resort to the psychological technique of denial in order to reassure themselves that they have nothing to worry about. In doing this they often find support from family, neighbours and friends, all of whom would prefer to avoid thinking about reality and hope for the best, as the saying goes. Sometimes this technique is successful because the anxieties denied in any case have no reality basis. Anxiety, however, has a habit of persisting, even in the face of strong denial, and it tends to gnaw away at the personality, sometimes manifesting itself in disguised forms such as physical or mental disorder.

The social worker is faced with the difficulty of deciding when it is appropriate to use reassurance as a technique for helping clients to deal with anxiety. The only circumstances in which its use may be unconditionally advocated are those where it is clear that there are no grounds for the anxiety, which can be explained away by the provision of factual information and concentration on reality. Thus a social worker may reassure a client that as a result of communicating with the housing department he has established that there is no possibility of eviction because of current rent arrears. Alternatively, he may find it preferable to offer reassurance in more tangible forms by arranging for individuals and groups to meet officials who can provide explanations that reduce anxiety, as when tenants are able to make contact with local government officers about matters of mutual concern. He may also accompany a client on a visit to a relative in a home, hospital or prison giving him the opportunity to see for himself the conditions which have perhaps given cause for concern.

When real grounds for anxiety exist, and the client persists in denying them, the social worker has to choose between two alternatives: colluding with the client's obvious need for reassurance or tackling the issue in a sensitive and realistic way which may initially produce pain and discomfort for the client, but which eventually may lead to a more satisfactory solution. In choosing to collude with the client by offering assurance to create false hopes, the social worker also protects himself from many immediate difficulties and like other professionals who face complex decisions, he may be tempted to do this. The social worker is sometimes in possession of knowledge to which the client is entitled and just as a doctor may refrain from telling a patient the true nature of his illness so a social worker may withhold information about relatives in order to protect and reassure. Saunders argues that 'So often people are not just protected from the truth that you are protecting them from; they are left alone with it instead',[7] making a strong case for complete honesty in dealing with patients and clients so that they receive all necessary help, but in reality it is a matter for fine judgement in individual situations. Ideally, it is preferable to help the client to acknowledge anxieties openly, introducing relevant knowledge and information where appropriate, in the hope that the sharing of feelings will produce a different kind of reassurance and the strength to cope with what was previously unacknowledged or overwhelming. In general, it may be said that false reassurance that seeks to mislead should be avoided but that in some situations, realistic reassurance may need to be accompanied by denial of some aspects of reality until the client is clearly ready to face up to them.

Promotion of self-understanding. One of the major contributions of psychoanalytic theory to the practice of social work has been the emphasis on insight as an essential element in emotional health. In particular, ideas about the importance of insight have permeated the literature about work with individuals and families to the point where it has come to be regarded as the most important aspect of social work intervention. More recently, writers such as Hollis[8] and Irvine[9] have questioned this view and suggested that the best social work is that which is most appropriate to the needs of the client, but insight is considered to be an important element in this. Insight is a somewhat difficult concept to grasp and at times this had led social workers to think that it lies in their power to give it to clients, when in reality it cannot be anything other than self-realisation and self-understanding. The promotion of self-understanding is therefore chosen as the most appropriate means of describing this aspect of social work intervention.

Many people go through life quite happily with the minimum of self-knowledge, so it is clearly no universal panacea. Others are only too well aware of their strengths and weaknesses, but find that this knowledge has little effect on their behaviour. As a first principle, therefore, it should never be assumed by social workers that the promotion of insight is desirable as an end in itself, nor that having achieved it, the client will necessarily behave differently. Nevertheless, there are some people who can be helped to act in a more responsible and intelligent manner if they are able to learn more about themselves, and the effect they have on others. The social worker has to use his judgement, based on knowledge of problems and past experience, to decide whether the promotion of self-understanding is an appropriate way of dealing with a client's problems. Because of the time required for what is usually a lengthy process, together with the obstacles and resistance likely to be encountered, this strategy perhaps more than any other is one about which a joint decision should be reached in discussion between social worker and client, prior to embarking on it. This is particularly important because there are some people for whom self-understanding is incapacitating rather than enabling.

At this point it is necessary to make clear what is and is not involved in self-understanding. Taking the latter first, it is not simply an intellectual acquaintance with one's condition, an ability to describe one's symptoms or problems in suitable jargon. This kind of knowledge is often displayed by people who have long experience of treatment by psychiatrists and social workers as a result of which they have learned the professional language and chosen their own labels, such as 'neurotic' or 'psychopath', which they then use as a form of explanation for their problems. True self-understanding is a dynamic process which never ceases and is therefore never complete. It involves the emotions as well as the intellect and is usually a difficult and painful process, because it entails the recognition and acceptance of those aspects of one's personality that it is preferable to hide and ignore. Before embarking on the promotion of self-understanding, therefore, the social worker should have a clear idea of why he wants to do it and should also be prepared to stop as soon as it has reached a satisfactory level for the client.

There is one further guideline which is of great importance and this lies in a distinction between two different levels of self-understanding. At one level, there is understanding related to the present, which helps clients or groups to see the effects of their behaviour on others. As they grow in understanding, so it is hoped that they will be able to modify their behaviour in ways that will elicit more favourable responses from others. This kind of self-understanding is of particular importance in work with marital pairs and families, in which increased awareness of the ways in which they treat each other may enable the people concerned to develop more satisfactory relationships. It can also arise in work with groups aimed at the exploration and elucidation of social relationships and in this form is used widely outside social work and psychiatry for training purposes in education, industry and elsewhere.

The second level of self-understanding involves insight into the origins and development of one's personality. This requires very detailed examination of past experiences and relationships, which may be re-lived in the present in the context of the relationship with the worker, a feature known as transference, because buried feelings towards parental and other figures are expressed in the relationship with the worker, who temporarily represents such personages. Work at this level is more characteristic of psychoanalysis than of social work, but at a less intense level social workers sometimes find themselves dealing with material from a client's past that is very much alive in the present. A common example of this arises in marital work, where events surrounding courtship, marriage and the attitudes of parents may still be highly influential twenty or more years later. Transference is discussed further in Chapter 9.

Although social work is a distinctive activity separate from psychoanalysis, there are certain overlapping areas between them, most noticeably in their mutual interest in promoting self-understanding. In psychoanalysis, however, this is a central feature, whereas in social work it is one of many strategies of intervention, selected on the basis of its appropriateness for particular clients. The link between the two is most clearly to be seen in what is known as psychotherapy. This is a form of treatment in which many of the classical elements of psychoanalysis are employed, but which also draws on some of the strategies used in social work intervention. The principal emphasis is on therapy through talking and listening, which links it closely, though not exclusively with the enabling aspects of social work. Psychotherapy, like casework, is used as a portmanteau term, and is not easily defined, as people use it in different ways. It is mentioned in this context because for some social workers it constitutes a special interest as a means of providing supportive, non-directive therapy to those prepared to discuss their problems regularly over a period of time, sometimes in a clinical, one-to-one relationship, sometimes in specially constituted groups. It is likely to remain a specialist interest because of the demands it makes on time and personnel and also because it is probably unsuited to many of the clients of social work agencies. There are nevertheless elements of psychotherapy to be found in the work of all social workers, who should therefore be aware of its existence.

7

Interpersonal Intervention

(ii) *Influencing and Creating*

Non-directiveness and self-determination are concepts that are treated with high regard in the practice of social work. In clinical situations, such as in psychotherapy, they may be exercised with relative freedom, as the worker usually possesses no official powers or responsibilities in relation to the client, who is himself theoretically free to act as he wishes. It has to be recognised, however that self-determination in life itself is limited for everyone by consideration of the needs and demands of others and it is acceptance of this fact that makes civilised society a possibility. Furthermore, relationships that become significant rarely lack elements of mutual influence between those concerned, so that however non-directive the social worker aims to be, in practice he must accept many limitations. His own words and behaviour are potential sources of change in the client, by whom he is also likely to be influenced himself. Finally, most social workers in Britain are charged with a variety of statutory responsibilities and these, together with the role they are often expected to play in maintaining social order, require the use of directive methods in practice. Nevertheless, even in the context of directiveness, the concept of self-determination is relevant in social work. Many clients of social workers fall into one of two opposite categories: those who are unable to exercise sufficient self-determination, such as the handicapped and the retarded, and those who appear to have indulged in an excess of it, such as the delinquent. In working with such people, there are two different kinds of objectives, in the one case aimed at increasing, in the other at reducing the level of self-determination. Neither in these situations, nor in those which fall in between, can the social worker pretend that his activities are entirely non-directive. Goal-directed social work in any case implies an element of direction of the client and even the providing and enabling strategies discussed in the preceding chapter are not carried out in a neutral context. Directiveness becomes even more apparent in considering strategies concerned with influencing and creating.

Influencing

The directive aspects of social work intervention are most clearly apparent in the use of strategies overtly designed to influence the behaviour of others. Social workers usually acknowledge that this is so in work done on behalf of clients, in which they seek to gain the support and help of other individuals and organisations in achieving the objectives in a case. They are often more reluctant to admit that in relation to clients themselves they are playing an influencing role, but as shown above, the nature of the social worker's task makes this unavoidable. This reluctance suggests that they may have a mainly negative view of influencing, forgetting that it permeates all relationships in life and is often beneficial in its outcome. As with all social work intervention, it is the latter aspect that is theoretically the more important one, though in practice influence may have to be exerted for less positive reasons in order to contain and control. Ideally, however, the use of influencing strategies is designed to contribute positively to the client's welfare. Such strategies may be used in mild and limited ways, but at times they are a substantial part of the action phase in social work, used to bring about major changes in the behaviour of individuals and groups.

Oversight. This term is used here to describe the many situations in which social workers are required to 'keep an eye' on people. It is a strategy very widely used in relation either to clients who are defined by society as being problems (such as offenders or neglected children), or to those who have sought and received help with some specific need but may want further assistance at some unspecified date in the future (such as patients discharged as recovered from a psychiatric hospital). Oversight usually takes the form of occasional visits or interviews, often of a fairly brief nature, in which the social worker seeks to reassure himself that all is well, though more active involvement to deal with specific problems may occur from time to time.

Evidence for the effectiveness of this strategy is difficult to find. It is presumably based on the rationale that minimal involvement is nevertheless sufficient to exert some positive influence on the client, perhaps as a reminder that he is expected to behave in certain ways (as in dealing with offenders on probation) and also possibly as a continuing indication that society is concerned about him. While these may be seen as potential benefits, the limitations are likely to be greater as the relationship with the social worker may be so tenuous that when real problems arise the client feels no confidence in the professional's ability to help and therefore does not consult him. In some senses, oversight is a means of deluding the social worker that he is actually doing something useful when he is not and this perhaps explains the existence of the enormous caseloads of elderly and handicapped clients accumulated by some departments, consisting of people known but rarely visited.

There are clearly people in society, such as the elderly, the blind and the handicapped, whose potential difficulties suggest that they need a form of continuing oversight if they are to manage the problems of daily living effectively, but it is doubtful whether a social worker is the best person to provide this service, except perhaps in cases where there is a statutory requirement obliging him to do so (as in probation work or the care of deprived children) and these usually require more than minimal contact. It therefore seems appropriate to encourage other services, such as home helps, meals on wheels and health visiting, to provide oversight in cases where they are involved in regular visiting and to develop more extensively the use of volunteers and neighbours for other situations that do not require the specialist help of a social worker. These other helpers would then be in a position to watch out for problems that seemed to require the social worker's help and make the appropriate referral when they arose.

Persuasion. Social workers are understandably reluctant to admit that their work often involves the use of persuasion and this word rarely makes an appearance in the literature. In particular, persuasion appears to be diametrically opposed to such principles as non-directiveness and self-determination. At its worst, it is seen as goading clients to alter their behaviour in ways that will satisfy the whims of the social worker and because of the negative connotations of persuasion and its widespread use in the fields of advertising and propaganda, it is right to be cautious about its relevance as a social work strategy. Nevertheless, it is evident from empirical observation that persuasion is an element in many of the activities of social workers and it therefore seems wise to recognise this honestly, with a view to ensuring that it is used responsibly.

There are three forms in which persuasion is most evident in social work practice: latent, manifest and coercive. *Latent* persuasion is present in all relationships between people in the sense that one person may be led to change his behaviour as a result of the example of another. This kind of influence is particularly likely to occur in relationships in which there is a strong element of authority or which are created for the specific purpose of helping one of the parties involved and these aspects are discussed in more detail in subsequent sections of this chapter. In the present context, it is sufficient to note that social work relationships frequently contain one or both of these elements and that the potential for persuasion is present, whether or not the social worker recognises and uses it consciously. The persuasive elements depend for their effectiveness on the way in which they provide a response to basic human needs. Thus clients often change their behaviour because they wish to please the social worker or because of the rewards, in terms of approval and praise, that are obtained thereby. Sometimes the social worker is seen as a model of what the client would like to become and that may also lead to modified behaviour which aspires to this ideal. It may be argued that many of the changes of behaviour engendered in this fashion are only temporary and that little long-term benefit can be achieved. That is certainly true in some cases, but the persuasive influences of personality and life-style are so apparent in society in general that it seems likely that in varying degrees clients may be able to take from relationships with social workers elements which substantially affect their future behaviour. For some clients, indeed, the social worker provides their first real experience of a stable and caring relationship and it would be very surprising if this was not a persuasive influence on their lives.

Manifest persuasion occurs where a social worker consciously attempts to bring about changes in the attitudes or behaviour of a client. It ranges from fairly straightforward situations in which, for example, a social worker tries to convince a client of the importance of paying the rent regularly, to complex problems involving a major life decision, such as when a frail elderly person is persuaded to give up his own home and enter a residential centre. It may also take the form of persuading people to avoid particular forms of behaviour, the focus of much work with offenders, who need to be convinced that it is in their interest to refrain from breaking the law. Equally, it may be applicable in work with a community group, when a social worker attempts to persuade the members that a public demonstration at a particular time would not be likely to contribute to the achievement of their objectives.

Underlying this form of persuasion is an assumption that most social workers prefer to reject: that they know what is best for other people. Although this approach is clearly false and pretentious if applied to all circumstances, there is nevertheless a certain amount of truth in it in two respects. First, there is often available clear objective data that if people behave in certain ways they are more likely to gain satisfaction in life for themselves and for others. This appeal to self-interest has relevance in such areas as paying the rent regularly and keeping out of trouble with the police, and one of the purposes of this kind of persuasion is to stimulate sufficient motivation in the client for a change of attitude or behaviour to occur. It sometimes happens that people are not aware of the rewards to be gained by a change of behaviour and here the social worker may be in a position to provide enlightenment as well as motivation. Thus a handicapped person who resists the idea of taking part in social activities with others similarly disabled may be persuaded to do so both by thorough discussion and by being taken on a trial visit to the local club.

Secondly, it is not presumptuous to claim that because of their knowledge and experience, social workers sometimes know better than the client what is likely to be beneficial. This is a difficult aspect to illustrate, since any example can be interpreted as a means by which social workers impose their own views on clients. In practice, however, social workers generally take care to examine all possible alternatives, giving the client the opportunity to choose which suits him best. Sometimes this means being content with allowing clients to continue living in squalor or unhappiness because that is what they choose, but such decisions should be made in the knowledge of other alternatives. This applies particularly to the elderly living alone and in the example given above it would be important to allow a frail person to remain in his own home, suitably supported by relevant social services, if that was what he really desired. It would also be important to give him the opportunity to visit a residential centre to which he could go permanently if he wished, and to emphasise the advantages which he might gain from doing so. Failure to discuss alternatives fully and to use persuasion appropriately may limit the client's opportunity to make a realistic decision and may thereby deny him the help he needs.

The *coercive* aspects of persuasion are an even greater source of discomfort for the social worker. In the first instance, he may feel himself under coercive pressure to treat a client in a particular way, as when relatives plead for a member of the family to be admitted to a psychiatric hospital or residential centre. He may also feel coerced by a law which is contentious and with which he is basically in disagreement. Thus he may believe that some forms of drug-taking should not be illegal, but be expected to persuade convicted offenders not to indulge, or he may feel under pressure to suggest abortion to a pregnant teenager although he has doubts about its morality. Even if these external pressures are not plainly evident, the social worker may be forced to resort to coercing clients as a last attempt to change their behaviour. Thus a social worker may tell parents who appear to be neglecting or ill-treating their children that they will be taken to court if they do not remedy the situation, or a probation officer may threaten action for breach of probation if an offender is lax in keeping to the conditions imposed on him. This is an uncomfortable but necessary aspect of the social worker's role, since it is one of the ways in which society provides protection for itself and for its weaker members. It is also likely to become increasingly important as attempts are made to replace custodial care in prisons and hospitals with supervision in the community. Finally, it is linked closely with the social worker's use of authority, discussed in a subsequent section of this chapter.

Confrontation. Most people would rather avoid than face up to the difficulties they encounter in life and they often resort to mechanisms such as denial and projection to escape from any sense of responsibility. Difficulties do not however disappear by being denied or blamed on to a convenient scapegoat and they have a way of recurring in aggravated form if not tackled and resolved when they first become apparent. In cases where there are strong psychological defences against facing reality, it is sometimes sufficient for social workers to use enabling techniques, which provide the security needed for the client to examine his difficulties honestly. For some clients, however, a more active approach is necessary and this is best described as confrontation.

In using confrontation strategy, the social worker aims to put before the client statements of how his behaviour appears to be affecting his own life and that of others. He may also indicate the likely nature of the consequences if the behaviour continues, such as marital breakdown or a prison sentence. This is the kind of reality that clients usually find unacceptable in normal circumstances, but which it may be important for them to face and tackle if they are to make beneficial changes in their lives. It is also the kind of reality that social workers may themselves prefer to ignore, colluding with clients in comfortable avoidance of the facts. Thus probation officers may sometimes forget that the principal reason for clients becoming their responsibility is an offence and that as long as there is a chance of further criminal activities occurring, this should be seen as one of the main problems to be faced and tackled. In dealing with complex family relationships or in working with groups it can also be helpful to adopt a confrontation strategy, in which the social worker brings out into the open what appear to be the ways in which people treat each other and the conflicts thereby engendered.

Confrontation, in fact, often implies conflict, and this is another aspect that social workers find uncomfortable because of their desire to promote harmony in relationships. It is important to see the expression of conflict and the influence thereby exerted on behaviour as one of the steps which can lead to greater harmony, both within the self and in relationships with others. It is also relevant to enabling strategies, particularly release of feelings (discussed in Chapter 6) and to the social worker's role in social action (discussed in Chapter 8). Although confrontation is obviously a much more drastic approach than using enabling strategies such as the promotion of self-understanding, there are some people who are better able to learn about themselves and their situation by being told how it appears to others than by being asked to think it out for themselves. As with every strategy, the use of confrontation is a matter for judgement based on skill and experience, but it is important to see it as a valid element in social work intervention, difficult though it may be to implement.

Authority and Control. The place of authority in social work practice continues to be hotly debated. There are those who argue that its use imposes serious limitations on the helping value of social work because of the constraints it puts on the client's freedom to be honest and open about himself. At the other extreme, there are those who see the presence of an element of authority as a vital ingredient of a dynamic social work relationship. In reality, there can be no relationships in social work that are utterly free of authority and it is more important to understand its different sources and to learn to use it effectively, than to quibble about its desirability or otherwise.

There are numerous sources for the social worker's authority. The law contributes by defining the status and powers of the social worker and enabling him to perform his work. Thus probation officers are invested with certain powers related to breach of probation orders and of parole conditions. Similarly, local authority social workers have certain statutory powers connected with the admission of mentally disordered people to psychiatric hospitals, together with legal obligations in relation to other need groups, such as children and young people. More generally, the law contributes to defining the structure, policies and procedures within which the social worker carries out his work which is further affected by local regulations and conditions. Similarly, there are legal and bureaucratic arrangements which control the power of social workers in regard to access to resources. This means that although they are rarely given absolute powers, social workers are sometimes in a strong position to influence the allocation of resources, such as places in residential centres for children or old people. They may also be able to influence the decisions made by other bodies, such as the courts and the local offices of the Supplementary Benefits Commission. Both of these aspects are discussed further in Chapter 8.

Another source of the social worker's authority is his knowledge and experience, which are part of his professional skill. The use of knowledge was discussed in Chapter 6, but to this must be added the growing authority of the social work profession as a whole. As numbers increase and standards of professional conduct become more clearly established, the reputation of social work adds to its authority. This contributes to the authority with which the client invests the social worker, because of his expectations about what can be obtained from him. It is important to note here that clients often credit social workers with much more authority than they actually possess and it becomes necessary to help them modify their expectations, as they learn about the limits on the social worker's power to take action on their behalf. Finally, there is the personal authority that each social worker develops in his own characteristic way and which permeates all of his relationships, with clients, with colleagues and with the staff of other agencies and organisations.

It should be obvious from the foregoing that authority is a facet of almost every strategy of intervention. In this section, discussion is focused on ways in which it may be used specifically as a strategy in itself. Although there are many possible variations, there are three main uses of authority as a strategy of intervention. The first is as a source of stability in relationships with clients For many people whose lives are chaotic and whose relationships tend to be transient, the authority of the social worker provides an anchor in that it is continuing, consistent and purposeful. The client 'knows where he is' in a way that is not possible in other areas of his life and for him the social worker becomes a reliable and authoritative person. There are obviously dangers of excessive dependence in such a relationship and these are discussed in Chapter 9. These dangers, however, have to be set against the benefits of a secure and supportive link with a professional person who knows what to do.

A second, and related aspect of the use of authority lies in the provision of control. The social worker sets limits to the behaviour of clients and expects them to be observed. In some situations, he is able to impose sanctions if he is disobeyed, as in dealing with offenders on probation. In working with a group, he may impose limits on the behaviour that is to be allowed at meetings and although these rules may have been devised initially by the group itself, he cannot absolve himself from the ultimate responsibility of enforcing sanctions. The use of control is of particular importance in residential care, where rules are essential to satisfactory group living and the social worker is expected to exercise authority in ways that are fair to all. The value of limits is that they not only provide boundaries for behaviour but also encourage a sense of security within the rules. There is much in all this that is connected with a 'parenting' role in social work. The good parent is one who not only loves the child but also sets the limits that enable him to grow up in a secure environment. Residential workers are particularly familiar with this role, but it is also one that is common in fieldwork and can be used constructively with adults as well as children with the objective of helping them to take more responsibility for managing their own lives.

The third use of authority in social work intervention is another dimension of the parental aspect. Many clients have negative and even hostile attitudes to authority, usually because they have hitherto experienced it only as a punitive element in their lives. This is often the result of unsatisfactory experiences with their own parents or with other significant figures in their lives, which they then transfer to attitudes to other people in authority over them. It can be extremely beneficial for such people to experience a relationship with a person in authority who is warm, kindly and understanding as well as firm and consistent. If they can come to appreciate that authority has caring as well as controlling aspects, they may learn to be less provocative in their dealings with officials and find that thereby they evoke a much more sympathetic response. The social worker thus tries to give a practical demonstration of a positive authority relationship, through which he hopes to induce changes in the client's attitudes. There is a further aspect to this, which is that through such an experience, the social worker is attempting to help the client to establish his own sense of authority as a person. It needs the use of enabling and other strategies to do this, as well as authority and control, since the development of self-confidence is a crucial factor in the creation of personal authority. Nevertheless, this kind of personal development can spring initially from learning to deal with authority in others. There are many examples of this to be found in community work, such as instances of individuals with poor self-esteem and an inadequately developed sense of their own authority who have overcome these handicaps by working on behalf of others and taking on leadership roles, with the encouragement of a social worker who provided the basic model of benevolent authority.

Behaviour Modification. Although a great deal of social work intervention involves attempts to modify behaviour, this has now become a specialism in its own right. Behaviour modification has developed in experimental and clinical psychology as a means of treating specific conditions, but its theoretical propositions[1] find support in the everyday practice of social workers, although many do not acknowledge this consciously. In brief, behaviour modification techniques are concerned with establishing clearly the nature of a problem, the resolution of which requires the use of specific and systematic treatment measures. As the name implies, the purpose is to bring about changes in behaviour, but it is also important that these changes should be observable and, where possible, measurable. Some methods involve the use of drugs and other aids that produce unpleasant effects when the client indulges in the behaviour which it is desired to change. Thus alcoholic addiction may be treated by means of drugs that make subsequent drinking of alcohol a highly unpleasant experience calculated to deter repetition. Negative techniques, however, are generally less favoured than those which evoke a positive response, either by reducing anxiety or by providing psychological rewards. For these to succeed, there must be clear agreement between client and therapist about the nature of the behaviour to be changed, together with sufficient motivation on the part of the client. Thus it has been found that phobias and some sexual disorders can be successfully treated in this way, by reducing the anxieties associated with them to a point where the difficulties themselves either disappear or can be dealt with more constructively by the client.

Behaviour therapists also place great emphasis on establishing warm and trusting relationships with clients as an essential basis for the application of the various techniques at their disposal. In this respect, they are interested in attempting to conceptualise the relationship 'more adequately and to identify the mechanisms by which it produces change'.[2] This is an aspect of behaviour modification that social workers have tended to ignore, believing that for the most part it can be carried out in the absence of a therapeutic relationship. The different techniques used in behaviour modification are fully described in the literature and it is not proposed to discuss them in detail in this context. It is important to note, however, that social workers use many of the techniques without realising that they are doing so, as when they assist parents to develop systematic methods of disciplining children and also more generally when they use praise and encouragement to reward positive and constructive efforts by the client, at the same time ignoring negative aspects in order to avoid reinforcing them.

Some social workers are now making more conscious use of behaviour modification techniques in the treatment of such conditions as enuresis and as awareness of its possibilities grows it seems likely that it will develop into a social work specialisation with close links with psychology. For other social workers behaviour modification raises ethical issues about the propriety of inducing changes in people's lives in so systematic and conscious a manner, which lead them to oppose its use. In adopting this attitude, however, they also seem to be denying the existence of influencing elements in the strategies of intervention used by all social workers, whatever their theoretical or ethical persuasion.[8] Alternatively, if they accept that influencing is involved in their own practice, they could be seen as asserting that it is less harmful and dangerous when used haphazardly and unsystematically, an extremely doubtful proposition. The most constructive attitude is to accept the reality of influencing strategies and to attempt to increase understanding of their application. Behaviour modification provides both a strategy in itself and a model for the introduction into social work practice generally of a greater emphasis on systematic approaches to assessment and intervention.

Creating

Although creating is placed last in this analysis of strategies of social intervention, it is in many ways the most important aspect, because it is fundamental to the successful use of providing, enabling and influencing strategies in social work practice. Social work has already been described as a blend of art and science, and it is in the area of creativity that the artistic elements predominate. This implies that social work is more than the application of commonly accepted techniques to definable situations, that social workers need imagination and skills to enable them to work effectively and that there are genuine elements of originality in social work practice. The creative aspects of social work are concerned with relationships and structures, with physical and psychological environments and with the provision of opportunities.

Relationships. The relationship with the client has often been described as the core of social work but some writers, including Mayer and Timms,[4] have begun to suggest that perhaps excessive emphasis is placed on its importance. Their research certainly indicated that the relationship sometimes seemed more important to the worker than to the client and that as a result, real problems remained unresolved while psychodynamic factors were explored. Nevertheless, this does not constitute an argument for dismissing the importance of relationships in social work. At a time when other professions, such as medicine and the law, are becoming increasingly aware of the importance of personal relationships and making efforts to improve the quality of their contacts with patients and clients, it would be unfortunate if social workers began to move away from this fundamental concern. Moreover, it is erroneous to infer from evidence that clients appear to be unaware of the importance of the relationship with the social worker that it is therefore of no significance at all. Subjective awareness is not the whole of perception, which operates at many levels of consciousness. Thus, although it is sensible for social workers to avoid over-emphasising the importance of the relationship at the expense of other aspects of social work intervention, it still provides the basis for effective practice and should be used constructively in the client's interests.

There are several different levels at which the relationship with the client may be used as a strategy in itself. To begin with, it must be clear that notwithstanding the professional and therefore contrived nature of most social work relationships, their effectiveness depends in large measure on the extent to which they are based on feelings of genuine interest and concern and on a desire by the social worker to understand the client. The response of the social worker to people who need help is ideally a receptive and accepting one, which demonstrates a caring attitude and through its warmth gives the client feelings of confidence and security. Without these elements, it is unlikely that any of the strategies previously discussed will be effective and it is also necessary to note that it is as important to maintain and nurture relationships as it is to create them.

The qualities mentioned above are as vital in short-term contacts as they are in work that continues over a longer peri time. In the case of isolated interviews with clients who are seen subsequently, it is perhaps especially important that th creative aspects of the relationship should be used effectively, to ensure that the maximum amount of help is given appropriately in a brief space of time. In many ways that is saying no more than that social workers need a kindly and sympathetic disposition, but since this characteristic is all too often lacking in the approach of officials of both public and private bodies in relation to their respective clientèles, it is clearly a quality that needs to be cultivated and developed through hard work and practice.

In medium and long-term work, it becomes possible to make use of relationships in more constructive ways. The first of these is the provision of what may be termed a 'good' relationship for clients who have experienced relationships in mainly negative ways hitherto. This good relationship provides security, trust, reliability and certainty to enable the client to begin work on his own difficulties and reach solutions for himself. Donald Winnicott, in his lectures to social work students on the treatment of disturbed children, talked of engaging in a holding operation, using the relationship to enable 'things to come together in some sort of integrated fashion'. Similarly, adults who are confused or bewildered may find that a relationship with a social worker provides them with sufficient sense of stability in one area of life to enable them to deal with some of the chaos elsewhere.

The third level in using relationships in social work requires more active involvement on the part of the worker. This is the promotion of personal growth through a relationship, the rationale for which springs from the approach to human development described by Storr.[5] This approach is based on a theory of personality growth as primarily the outcome of experience in relationships, particularly in the family, but later in life including those with significant others, such as teachers, youth leaders, clergy and then husbands and wives. In this sense, a social worker may become a significant other in the life of a client and he thus has opportunities to use his own personality to stimulate the growth process. The client takes from the relationship what he needs at the time, including elements that he may later discard as no longer important, but if the relationship has been a significant one, traces of its effects remain permanently. Work with groups adds further dimensions to this process by providing opportunities for clients to learn from relationships with each other as well as with the social worker and this can be a particularly valuable approach for those such as adolescents who may feel more comfortable with their peers than with older people. The use of relationships is closely connected with the influencing strategies discussed in the first part of this chapter and in fact permeates the whole of social work practice. Further discussion of the nature of social work relationships and the skills involved in using them will be found in Chapters 9 and 10.

Structures. Wherever social work takes place, be it in an office, in the client's home, in a residential or day centre, or anywhere else, its goal-directed nature requires the creation of a suitable structure to enable effective work to be done. It is the social worker's responsibility to do this by organising his time and planning his work appropriately. This involves making decisions about the nature of the contact he has with clients, its frequency, duration and the venue for their meetings. It is often possible to reach agreement about these matters in discussion with clients, but it is the social worker who must take the initiative, if necessary insisting on regularity of appointments as an aid to effective work. Thus, for example, the resolution of marital problems usually requires frequent meetings and the social worker should make this clear when establishing with a couple how their difficulties might best be tackled. Clients should also be involved in decisions about where meetings take place and who should be involved as participants, although once again the social worker must often take the initiative himself in suggesting what seem likely to be the best arrangements, for example office interviews in preference to home visits.

In working with groups, the need for a basic structure becomes even more apparent. Allowing for individual preferences which provide a degree of flexibility, there is nevertheless a considerable amount of knowledge derived from experience about ideal minimum and maximum numbers in a group, depending on its purpose. It is also necessary to make decisions about whether the group membership should remain unchanged or whether new members can be admitted from time to time and if there is to be a set number of meetings rather than continuation with no limit fixed in advance. In the community context, the social worker may have to decide at what point to call a meeting, whom to invite and how to set about furthering the business in hand by use of subsequent gatherings in the form of committees, working parties and ad hoc groups. In creating structures that make it possible for desired outcomes to be achieved, the social worker's knowledge and experience provide the basis for offering relevant advice and taking appropriate decisions.

Aspects of structure are also related to the content of interviews and meetings. This is a matter that requires careful planning and preparation if time and other resources are to be used to best effect. Thus interviews with individuals must be structured so that discussion is not a social conversation but is focused on the essential aspects of the problem in hand. Similarly, group meetings must be planned and committees require agendas if they are to fulfil their objectives. Although it is sometimes necessary to abandon carefully prepared plans because of changes in the client's situation or the demands of a crisis which must take precedence, this does not diminish the importance of devising structures that enable effective work to be done. With experience, this can be done on a flexible basis that allows the social worker to make suitable modifications speedily in response to changed circumstances, thus providing an alternative structure for the new situation. Finally, the creation of a structure is an important element in the overall action plan for an individual or group. Any such plan may involve deliberate changes in the context of the case, as, for example, when a client living with his family moves into residential care in order to receive treatment or follow a rehabilitation programme. It may also involve changes in the dimension of social work, as, for example, when group work is substituted for individual work as an attempt to meet needs more appropriately in a particular case.

The Physical Environment. Social work is carried out in physical surroundings which are often taken for granted, but which have nevertheless been provided for specific purposes. This is obvious in the case of residential and day centres, but it also applies to office accommodation, including interviewing facilities and meeting rooms. In both field and residential work, the physical facilities often seem woefully inadequate in both quantity and quality and much effort is rightly expended in trying to effect improvements. Seen in terms of social work strategy, however, the important aspect is the effective use of whatever physical resources are available, however inappropriate or inadequate they may appear to be.

The use of the physical environment is often a fairly minor adjunct to the employment of other strategies, but it can nevertheless be of importance to the well-being of the client that he is able to sit in a comfortable chair in a peaceful room, where he can receive the undivided attention of the social worker. It may also be important that the social worker sits at the same level as the client and does not retreat behind a desk, as this emphasises that the approach is one of professional caring rather than of bureaucratic officialdom. Similar considerations apply to the creation of an appropriate physical environment for meetings of groups and committees, including the arrangement of chairs in ways that facilitate rather than inhibit communication. Thus it is preferable for all present to be able to see each other face to face and a circular arrangement in particular helps to emphasise ideas of democracy and equality. The creation of a suitable physical environment is therefore a basic strategy in social work, as it often provides a foundation for the use of other interventive methods.

The environment itself may also be used as a central strategy in helping a client. This applies particularly to residential and day centres, where the main emphasis of care may well be on physical comfort and the availability of a range of activities to match the interests of the individuals concerned. Examples of this may be found in homes for the elderly, some small family group homes for children, day centres for the physically handicapped and training centres for the mentally handicapped, and in the wide variety of clubs and community centres, where the emphasis is on shared enjoyment of the physical environment. It takes effort and imagination to create a comfortable and supportive physical environment, for this requires attention to small matters, such as the presence of pictures and vases of flowers, as well as to more substantial provisions, such as billiard tables and television sets. It is also easy to be distracted from a creative role by the demands of cleanliness and tidiness, which have a tendency to develop into primary rather than secondary aims if sufficient self-control is not exercised by the staff involved. Finally, for some clients the performance of useful work is an important element in the physical environment. In training centres for the mentally handicapped work is a central feature of the daily routine but clients in other centres sometimes benefit from the opportunity to share in essential tasks such as cooking, washing-up and gardening. Where such involvement is felt to be inappropriate, occupational therapy and educational activities provide alternative means of engaging in creative work.

The Psychological Environment. Although the physical environment may at times be the predominant concern of the social worker, particularly in residential and day care, the nature of the social work task generally requires a similar focus on the psychological environment. This includes the attitudes of individuals to their work; the relationships between different members of staff and between staff and clients. Although these aspects may be much more apparent in work with groups and in residential and day care, they also have relevance to the individual social worker and his client, since his attitudes and approach are influenced by the relationships within his working environment. When these are positive and supportive, the client will feel the benefit transmitted to him in terms of the social worker's concentration and undivided concern. When they are less good, the client may feel a lower degree of confidence in the social worker.

The promotion of a supportive and facilitating environment is of crucial importance in residential and day care, in which social workers and clients are engaged in treatment which goes beyond simply providing somewhere for a person to live and interact with others. It is also one of the most difficult aims to achieve, even with the help of the many other workers who are often involved, such as nurses, teachers, occupational therapists and domestic staff. It requires all concerned to work together collaboratively in pursuance of the overall goal and also to change and adapt their methods so that the quality of the psychological environment is maintained at a level that is capable of managing rather than being destroyed by the conflicts that inevitably arise in group interaction. At its best, it is found in the working of hospitals, hostels and other institutions that have set themselves up as therapeutic communities, in which there is open and frank discussion of individual and group problems, usually on a carefully planned and structured basis, with considerable blurring of role distinctions between professionals and clients and also among the different professionals, such as doctors, nurses and social workers, who may be involved. The therapeutic community is an attempt to break away from an older, hierarchical model of residential care characterised by authoritarian attitudes and to involve the patient or client more actively in the treatment process designed to help him. Although in its most intense forms it may be appropriate only for particular types of institution dealing with distinctive problems, such as psychiatric hospitals, schools for maladjusted children and various small hostels, there are aspects of the idea of the therapeutic community which are relevant for all types of work with groups, whether residential or not. These are the emphasis on democratic decision-making through client participation, the involvement of clients in the maximum amount of self-help consistent with their physical and psychological abilities and the need for staff to work together in active co-operation on the basis of shared goals in mutually supportive relationships.

Although these ideals are infrequently achieved in practice, they serve to emphasise the importance of the psychological environment in social work intervention. They imply that the social worker should consciously make use of individual and group relationships to promote the well-being of clients. They are also relevant to all situations, whether or not some kind of treatment programme is involved, so that even when the predominant purpose is the provision of social facilities or a substitute home, staff should be aware of ways in which they can together create an integrated and constructive psychological environment.

Opportunities. The creation of opportunities is an aspect of social work intervention that largely depends on work in the environment of the various kinds discussed in Chapter 8. There are, however, two ways in which the creation of opportunities is relevant to interpersonal intervention. The first of these is as an alternative to the more usual methods, in situations where the social worker, recognising that he alone is unable to meet all the needs of the client, takes steps to introduce other elements that may be of relevance. This is most likely to happen where groups of people are involved. Thus the social worker may help a group to form in order to bring together people whom he thinks may help each other or who may engage in shared activities that provide new experiences for each member. Where activities are concerned, they may be purely recreational or they may alternatively be specifically related to the individually assessed needs of the members. In the latter category come such activities as psycho-drama and socio-drama in which, through the playing of roles, the members of the group develop greater understanding about themselves and their relationships with others. It is not wise to engage in such specialised group work without adequate training and preparation, but it is included here as an aspect of intervention worthy of further development. In the community context, the social worker is concerned to bring people together so that they may create opportunities for themselves and others, as for example in the development of a neighbourhood centre or an adventure playground. By enabling the appropriate people to come together as a group, the social worker is also creating for them the opportunity to take action on their own behalf. He may also achieve similar results in working with individuals, using information, advice, material aid, encouragement and other strategies to create for the client an opportunity to achieve greater successes in life, whether in relationships or in academic or practical tasks.

The second way in which the creation of opportunities is relevant to interpersonal intervention arises from the broader approach to the treatment of social problems that is now endorsed in legislation. In particular, schemes involving intermediate treatment and community service for offenders place on local authority social workers and probation officers an obligation to create new approaches to problems previously dealt with largely on an individual basis by professionals on their own. Schemes must now be devised that provide opportunities for the creative development of individuals either in groups of their peers or in association with members of the public in which they engage in useful forms of service. If these schemes are to be successful, they must be seen as involving more than simply finding something for people to do. A great deal of work is required, both with the client, to discover the nature of his interests and his creative potential, and with any members of the community who wish to be actively involved, so that they are adequately prepared for their roles.

Although these ideas may seem novel, they are little more than an extension of what is established practice in other areas of social work. In particular, the staff of day and residential centres have long been concerned with creating opportunities for the clients with whom they deal. Such opportunities involve education, work and recreation, and a successful centre is usually one that has an imaginative blend of all three adapted to the particular needs of the clients with whom it is concerned. Finally, although a somewhat elusive concept, it is worth noting that in many ways all forms of social work are about creating and increasing opportunities for those who are deprived by physical, emotional and social handicaps of the achievement of their full potential and have often as a consequence been dismissed as incapable of further development.

8

Environmental Intervention

When studies are made of the ways in which social workers spend their time, surprise is usually expressed at the small proportion that is devoted to face-to-face contacts with clients. This generally proves at most to be about one-third of the working time available, a finding which readily leads to frustration on the part of social workers who interpret it as an indication that they are being prevented by other forces, usually bureaucratic, from making full use of their professional skills in direct work with clients. It is therefore important to recognise that the provision of an effective social work service requires other activities besides face-to-face work with clients and to accept these as a valid part of the professional task. These other activities include administration (discussed in Chapter 11), consultation (discussed in Chapter 12), and a wide range of work carried out on behalf of clients that may be conveniently described as environmental intervention.

In environmental intervention, the social worker is concerned to involve both individuals and systems within the social structure in the process of providing service to the client. To be effective in this capacity the social worker requires an extensive knowledge, particularly of welfare provisions, a sensitive awareness of which individuals and organisations are likely to co-operate in ways that will benefit the client and a conception of his role which goes beyond helping individuals and groups to encompass a general concern for the well-being of society, this being a crucial element in determining the quality of services available for the client's benefit. These three requirements are implicit in each of the strategies of environmental intervention discussed below.

Working with 'Significant Others'. 'Significant others' is a clumsy but useful term to describe the great variety of people on whom the well-being of a client may depend and with whom it may therefore be important for the social worker to be involved. Such people fall into two groups: relatives and friends of the client, and the social worker's fellow professionals, using that term in a very broad sense.

In the model of social work intervention set out in Chapter 5, it was indicated that the family forms one of the dimensions for the social work approach, but there are many situations in which it is not possible to tackle family difficulties by working with the family as a whole. Various members may be living apart, there may be tensions and conflicts among those living together, the client may be a scapegoat for whom relatives wish to absolve themselves of responsibility, or the only known relatives may be distant ones only brought into the picture by the advent of sudden illness or disability. In working with relatives, the social worker's first aim is naturally to help the client and this sometimes requires the adoption with them of various strategies of interpersonal intervention, as discussed in preceding chapters. Thus, for example, he may use persuasion to bring about a change of mind on the part of people who want an elderly relative taken into residential care, or he may provide information to help parents understand more fully the problems of a wayward adolescent. In some senses, work of this kind with relatives might be described as a liaison role, but as has already been indicated it sometimes extends beyond this to the use of interpersonal strategies. In these circumstances it becomes appropriate for relatives themselves to be given the status of clients, to enable them to receive help on a broad basis, rather than simply in relation to the problems of another member of the family who was the first person to be referred for help. A good example of this is the mentally handicapped child who needs much help himself, but whose parents also require assistance, though of a different kind.

When relatives are few or distant, it can be important for social workers to establish contact with friends or neighbours of the client and once again there are two aspects to this role, liaison and direct help. Work with friends and neighbours is especially important in cases where people at risk, such as the physically handicapped or the less able-bodied elderly, are living alone and may need help at unpredictable times. In such situations, as sometimes in working with relatives, the social worker's aim is to build up supportive elements in the environment of the client. This not only ensures that emergencies will receive speedy attention but provides him with a means of referral if friends and neighbours are willing to tell him when his presence is needed to provide direct help to the client.

In the absence of friends and neighbours able to provide a client with support, social workers sometimes attempt to introduce other helpers in the form of volunteers, in the hope that friendships will develop that complement the professional one and thereby do more to counteract loneliness and isolation. Volunteers have always played a significant role in the provision of social services but have sometimes been viewed with suspicion by professionals anxious to establish their own position. Such negative attitudes are less apparent now that it is more accepted that volunteers are not amateur social workers but fulfil a helping role that is different from and complementary to that of the professional. Since 1973, there has been a national Volunteer Centre in London charged specifically with the task of promoting the use of volunteers in social welfare throughout Britain. The work of the Centre, together with the activities of voluntary organisations and voluntary workers' bureaux throughout the country, undoubtedly means that volunteers will become an increasingly significant feature in the interventive strategies devised by social workers.

Many volunteers work informally and their presence may be unknown to social workers visiting the same individuals and families. Other volunteers are deliberately recruited by social work agencies to undertake tasks for which they are thought to be specially suited. Thus, in the probation and after-care service, volunteers work with offenders on an individual basis and have shown themselves to be particularly valuable in helping men and women who have served sentences in penal institutions. Other probation and after-care volunteers have been involved in the provision of group activities for prisoners' wives. These volunteers occupy a fringe position between relatives and friends and the professional social worker. At best, they provide a highly supportive relationship together with greater frequency of contact with the client than social workers' caseloads normally permit, but it is usually found that they themselves need help and encouragement if they are to maintain their interest and persevere. Thus the social worker must work closely with the volunteer and be prepared to offer guidance where appropriate, including opportunities for group discussion with other volunteers, a particularly helpful means of support in the experience of many agencies. Some so-called volunteers, such as foster-parents, are virtually professionals in their own right, but this does not reduce their need for support, both individually and in group meetings, for their work is often exceptionally difficult and taxing. In professional and para-professional relationships, whether with colleagues or volunteers, it is important for social workers to recognise that support is often a two-way process in which both parties stand to gain in understanding of their work.

The social worker's fellow professionals include both his own colleagues and those doing related work which may impinge on the welfare of clients. Among the latter are numbered doctors, lawyers, clergy, police, teachers, youth leaders and sometimes employers, any of whom may have significance in the lives of clients. The list is by no means exhaustive but it is less important to name every group that might be involved than to emphasise that each has its own view of people and its own value system, either of which may or may not accord with that of the social worker. Moreover, within each group there are individual differences that run parallel to those found within the social work profession itself. It is vital that social workers should be aware of these potential differences among professionals who play significant roles in the lives of clients. Rather than dismissing them as irrelevant or counter-productive, the social worker needs to develop skills in working constructively with a wide range of workers with differing attitudes, where possible co-ordinating their efforts to produce the best possible service for the client. Such skills require the ability to work in conflict as well as in consensus situations and also the humility to accept that social workers, like any other professionals, are not infallible.

Mobilisation of Community Resources. To the extent that his fellow professionals are themselves community resources, one of the aims of the social worker is to ensure that clients obtain their service when appropriate. The mobilisation of community resources, however, involves a broader approach that extends beyond individuals to departments and organisations. In some situations, the necessary resources can be supplied by the social worker's own employing department. Social services departments are empowered to provide a wide range of resources to meet need, including the assistance of the social worker himself, but extending beyond that to encompass various other specialised types of help. Thus the social worker may make arrangements for clients to receive services in their homes, such as domestic help or meals on wheels; or for adaptations to be made to a house, such as additional stair rails and widened doors, to enable a physically handicapped person confined to a wheelchair to continue living in his own home. Outside the home, the social worker may make arrangements for day care at a club, day centre or workshop, or for temporary or permanent accommodation at a residential centre. Most departments also have a range of other provisions and resources which can be used as appropriate, such as holiday schemes for the elderly and handicapped and domiciliary occupational therapy services.

Outside his employing department, there are other local authority departments which provide resources on which the social worker often needs to call, notably in the spheres of housing and education. These, together with the facilities of national organisations, such as the National Health Service and the Social Security and Employment services, are major providers within the social welfare system, with whose services the social worker must be fully acquainted if he is to help clients obtain the benefits to which they are entitled. Similarly, the social worker must be familiar with and understand the work of other bodies whose activities impinge on the lives of clients, such as the courts, local councils, community relations councils and all the other statutory and voluntary bodies that may be concerned.

In attempting to mobilise community resources, the social worker usually aims to ensure that clients obtain fair treatment and get what is their rightful entitlement. The only exception to this arises in dealings with courts of law, where the social worker acts as an adviser to those who actually make the decisions and is not expected to engage in pleading for the defence, which is the responsibility of the client or his counsel. Even in court, however, the social worker is often expected to provide a solution to the problem of sentence or disposal and except in circumstances where the nature of the crime dictates a deterrent or frankly punitive dispensation, those sitting in judgement increasingly aim to make decisions that accord with the welfare of the offender. The social worker is usually the principal adviser on welfare aspects and is therefore concerned to encourage the court to take the course that is in the client's best interests.

It is useful to make a distinction between those community resources that are theoretically available to all who qualify for them and those which are limited in supply or are subject to the exercise of discretion by officials. In the former category are social security benefits to which there is an entitlement by right, such as family allowances or retirement pensions, but for which lack of knowledge sometimes acts as a barrier to receipt. Here the social worker should be able to draw the attention of the appropriate department to any anomaly and ensure that it is corrected. When the supply of resources is limited or discretionary, the social worker may take on the role of advocate and plead on behalf of his client for a particular form of assistance to be provided. To do this effectively, he needs accurate and detailed information, together with skill in presenting a convincing case. If the resources are limited, as is usual, for example, in accommodation in residential centres, he may well be competing with colleagues for access to the same provision and a process of negotiation or bargaining becomes necessary. The guiding principle here is clearly that those most in need should get the highest priority, but it is exceptionally difficult to apply this standard fairly in the absence of objective criteria. As a result, social workers have to accept failures in advocacy and seek other means of solving the client's predicament. Although advocacy extends beyond individual cases to act as an influence on policy, resources are unlikely ever to be so freely available that questions of priority and negotiation become irrelevant.

Discretionary benefits provide the social worker with other kinds of difficulty. The justification for such benefits is that they enable individual need to be dealt with in a flexible manner that is related to a specific situation, but discretion may also be used to withhold resources and protect the public purse. Stevenson[1] demonstrates the conflict of attitudes involved by distinguishing between 'proportional' and 'creative' justice. Public bodies, such as the Supplementary Benefits Commission, operate largely on the basis of proportional justice, in which fair treatment is seen as everyone with similar needs being treated in the same way. Social workers are more interested in creative justice that is flexible enough to meet individual needs even though it results in different treatment for apparently similar situations. This conflict is the basis for the social worker's use of advocacy as a means of helping his clients, but there are differences of opinion within the profession about the extent to which this technique should be carried. To plead a cause effectively, whether it be for a small payment to an individual to cover extra heating costs or for a substantial amount of money to be made available for the repair of deteriorating houses on an estate, it is necessary to believe in and be fully identified with the needs of the client. This implies that the social worker must sometimes step aside from his usual balancing role between the client and society and take sides to some extent, in the process of which he may engender conflict between himself, his employers and other departments. It would be unrealistic to assume, therefore, that all advocacy takes place in an atmosphere of consensus and the individual social worker has to decide for himself at what point he will move into open conflict and all the risks it entails.

Social Action. Social action is a further extension of the advocacy role and it was perceived as an increasingly significant aspect of social work in the chapter of the Seebohm Report which dealt with 'The Community'.[2] It was recognised in that chapter that in working on behalf of his clients, the social worker might sometimes find it necessary to be critical of local authority policies and practices, among them those of his own employing department. Authorities and individuals in positions of authority rarely find it easy to accept criticism and usually respond to it defensively in an attempt to undermine its source or minimise its importance, rather than being prepared to examine it rationally to see if it contains anything of value. An individual social worker engaging in social action, whether fighting for one client or family, using publicity in the media or participating with a community group on a march or at a demonstration, is particularly vulnerable and liable to lose all credibility if he cannot justify his position and gain the support of professional colleagues. It therefore seems likely that the most effective forms of social action are those engaged in by social workers as a group and such evidence as there is from practice seems to support this view. Thus on one occasion social workers in Islington openly aligned themselves with a group of squatters in opposition to the policy of the local council which employed them and do not appear to have suffered unduly as a consequence.[3]

It is also useful to distinguish between different levels of social action. The type which has been discussed so far is concerned with local issues affecting an individual, group or community and is usually specific in nature. At local level, social workers are also involved in a great deal of legitimate social action, which does not require conflict strategies. Much of the work in community development, in which social workers attempt to help local people understand and find solutions to their own problems, involves assisting groups in social action as part of the process, for example in mounting a campaign to promote interest in the establishment of an adventure playground. Similarly, social workers are frequently involved in activities designed to increase the range and availability of community resources, as in campaigns to recruit volunteers or in committee work aimed at producing better facilities for particular need groups. In connection with the latter, it is important for social workers to involve themselves in discovering ways in which they can influence the policies of their own agencies. This area of social action tends to be neglected because of the apparent difficulty of inducing change in bureaucratic systems and its potential therefore remains largely unexplored. These points are further discussed in Chapter 12.

Finally, there is social action directed at national policies. Some would argue that much of the ameliorative work of social workers is wasted because so many of the problems faced by clients spring from national and even international forces arising from complex economic and technological factors over which the individual has little control. Thus, the social worker may be able to do little to remedy individual poverty or unemployment and, so the argument goes, should concentrate primarily on attempting to change the established system, including the structure of society itself. The importance of a national approach to major problems is demonstrated in the experience of the community development projects sponsored by the Home Office.[4] These were originally designed to find new ways of dealing with local problems on a more integrated basis at local level, but it very quickly became apparent that many of the issues that arose, such as unemployment, poverty, and inadequate housing, were interconnected and influenced by national factors which could only be tackled at national level. The project workers thus turned their attention to devising ways of influencing national policies, and although local issues and solutions were not abandoned entirely, the relevance of these findings from the community development projects for social workers engaging in community action is clear. Purely local issues may appropriately be dealt with locally, but national problems require a broadly based national approach that involves many other individuals and organisations besides social workers.

Public Education. Campaigns promoted by social workers are rarely popular. They are carried out on behalf of stigmatised and scapegoated groups, which evoke strong criticism from those apparently able to manage their affairs successfully without needing to resort to welfare benefits. If the minorities for whom the social worker is concerned are to be adequately cared for and helped, it is necessary for the comfortable majority to become interested in their plight and willing to act sympathetically towards them. This is where public education is relevant and provides many opportunities for social workers to further the causes in which they are interested. Opportunities for public education arise in various ways. There are the individual contacts made from day to day with employers, teachers and other significant members of the community, all of whom may be helped through discussion to understand more fully the problems of someone known to them whose troubles have brought him on to the social worker's caseload. There are many examples of individual citizens whose interest has been evoked in this way, leading them into active work themselves in a voluntary capacity.

Social workers are frequently asked to speak at meetings of all kinds of local organisations, both educational and recreational, and here they have an opportunity both to inform and to inspire. Once again, these situations sometimes lead to interest being actively expressed in valuable work undertaken voluntarily by individuals and groups. Adult education centres provide opportunities for more formal education of the layman about social welfare and social work and this is one of the ways in which former practitioners who have become teachers of social work can continue to further the aims of the profession. Finally, it is important to emphasise the importance of the mass media, notably newspapers, radio and television. These are particularly valuable in community work, in which there are many examples of constructive uses of publicity, but they might also be more extensively employed by statutory departments, whose responsibilities and activities are often misunderstood or simply not known. For this very purpose, some statutory departments have appointed information officers who are able to maintain contact with representatives of the mass media and thus keep the public informed about policies and developments.

Perhaps the most effective form of education is through participation. Opportunities to involve the public in the provision of social services sometimes arise naturally in the course of the public education activities of the social worker, as when a group he has addressed ask what they can do to help. Such opportunities should be seized and used, but they also arise in other ways, often through the performance of statutory duties. This applies especially to those duties which cannot be carried out effectively without community participation, such as intermediate treatment programmes for young people and community service schemes for offenders. In the course of making arrangements for such schemes, the social worker has the opportunity not only to meet and educate members of the public, but also to invite their participation in active ways, in such roles as instructors, guides or supervisors. Such participation inevitably evokes interest and a desire to involve others, so that in educating members of the public the social worker is initiating a process of permeation within the community, ultimately designed to promote more understanding and sympathetic attitudes to those who become social casualties.

Promotion of Social Change. In the discussion of social action, reference was made to the social worker's concern with social change. It would no doubt be difficult to arrive at complete agreement among social workers with regard to the kind of social change that is desirable, but most would accept that if there is any logic at all in the aims of social work, they imply social as well as individual change, a point that was discussed in considering the basis of social work in Chapter 1 of this book. The changes are usually described in terms of more equal distribution of resources, greater equality of opportunity in every sphere and special discrimination in favour of those in greatest need. Social work is thus a progressive rather than conservative profession and its commitment is a firmly political one that can be identified with a radical view of the world. It certainly no longer seems possible to be concerned with the welfare of the individual without taking account of the systems and structures which impinge on his life. Some might want to dispute this argument on the grounds that social work must be non-political if it is to maintain its integrity, but it is difficult to sustain this view now that the profession's focus has broadened from the individual and the family to the community as a whole. Social work is now concerned with improvements for all, but its special interest in the needs of the underprivileged implies a political stance. Moreover, it is likely to be one that is more often in opposition to than in agreement with the prevailing political forces, because in an imperfect society there are always new issues demanding new solutions.

Some social workers decide to carry their political views into party membership and some become local councillors. There are problems arising from identification with a particular political party, especially in the sphere of community work, where the group represented may lose credibility and effectiveness among councillors of different opinions. Moreover, if its representative is unseated at a subsequent election, the local group may find that its voice is no longer heard in the political arena, suffering a setback from which it may take a long time to recover. Social workers interested in active party political work have to weigh these potential losses against the gains they expect to accrue from such a public stance. It is also possible to limit political involvement to party membership which provides an opportunity to participate in policy formulation at both local and national levels. This is an area of possible influence that social workers are perhaps prone to neglect.

Other social workers, equally concerned about social change, prefer to express their concern without becoming aligned with a political party. In pursuance of this, they may use their membership of a professional association, such as the British Association of Social Workers, the National Association of Probation Officers, the Association of Community Workers or the Residential Care Association, all of which are bodies that exert pressure on matters that concern them in the political field. Social workers also involve themselves actively with the work of pressure groups such as Shelter, the Child Poverty Action Group and Radical Alternatives to Prison, as another means of social and political action.

There are thus many ways in which a commitment to social change may be expressed. As with most of the strategies discussed in this chapter, the client sometimes appears to be rather remote because the work involved takes place on his behalf and affects him only indirectly. There is no doubt that direct work with clients is the predominant concern of social workers, and it is right that this should be so, because the client is the person in need at a specific point in time and the social worker is one of the professionals appointed by society to render him help. That understood, however, there remain implications for society as a whole, which can be mediated by the social worker to the policy makers. Social workers are not alone in being concerned about social change, but the nature of their work with the disadvantaged and underprivileged provides them with much relevant information on which to base campaigns for social improvement.

Strategies of Social Intervention—Conclusion

In this chapter and the two preceding it, social work methodology has been divided into twenty-two strategies of intervention, which are summarised in the table below. The scheme is set out in this way to help social workers to understand more clearly what is involved in their work and to enable them to make clear choices about appropriate strategies in each case. As has already been suggested, strategies are rarely used in isolation, but it is important that they should be applied as a planned programme of intervention in which the individual elements complement each other. Strategies that are likely to be counter-productive if used in combination should thus be avoided. For example, material aid may well be incompatible with the promotion of self-understanding, although the one might precede the other in a planned programme of intervention.

By using this scheme of strategies in conjunction with the process model of social work outlined in Chapters 3 and 4, social workers should be able to direct their efforts more economically and appropriately in their work. There are no strategies that are never relevant, whatever the context and dimension of social work, but they should be used differentially according to the requirements of defined needs and established goals.

TABLE II: STRATEGIES OF SOCIAL INTERVENTION

Interpersonal Intervention	*Environmental Intervention*
Providing	Working with Significant Others
Information and Advice	Mobilisation of Community Resources
Material Aid	Social Action
Education	Public Education
	Promotion of Social Change
Enabling	
Release of Feelings	
Clarification	
Encouragement	
Promotion of Self-Understanding	
Influencing	
Oversight	
Persuasion	
Confrontation	
Authority and Control	
Behaviour Modification	
Creating	
Relationships	
Structures	
The Physical Environment	
The Psychological Environment	
Opportunities	

9

Relationships in Social Work

(i) *Characteristics and Phases*

The reader who has persevered this far should now understand something of what is involved in the practice of social work. He should appreciate that it is a process that takes place over a period of time, however brief, and that it involves the selection and use of strategies appropriate to the needs of the client and the objectives chosen. As such, the reader resembles a person who has been presented with a kit of unfamiliar equipment which, while it may excite his interest, is nevertheless deficient by reason of the absence of one vital component, the instructions on how to use it. This chapter and the three that follow it are designed to remedy that deficiency by focusing on the 'how' of social work practice, but it must be said at the outset that this aspect of social work is probably the most difficult to write about with clarity and precision. New recruits to social work training often have an expectation that they will be told in lectures and tutorials exactly how to do their work in the right way, but the reality is that such skills must be acquired through practice and experience, rather than in classroom instruction.

A further complication is the difficulty of separating the 'how' and the 'what' of social work practice, since the two are so closely interwoven. In discussing strategies, it was impossible to avoid references to skills: likewise, in analysing skills, it will be necessary to make references here and there to strategies. A skill is usually defined in terms of expertise, involving complex operations carried out as a result of practice, and in social work the need for expertise is apparent in three main areas: relationships (discussed in this chapter and the one that follows it), transactions (discussed in Chapter 11) and working in an organisational context (discussed in Chapter 12). It may be argued that since all human beings differ from each other, there can be little that is of general relevance to all, but it is also true that they are more alike than unalike, so that skill involves a capacity to be adaptable rather than completely different, modifying reactions, responses and strategies to suit individual situations. In the discussion of skills which follows, it will be seen that adaptability and flexibility are fundamental to effective social work intervention.

Characteristics of Social Work Relationships

The creation of relationships was discussed in Chapter 7 as one of the strategies of interpersonal intervention, but skill in relationships permeates the whole of social work practice and is one of the essential attributes of the social worker. In particular, it is vital that the social worker should be able to establish effective working relationships with clients and others as a foundation for achieving the objectives of intervention. The principal reason for stressing this aspect is that social work is practised mainly through talking and listening, in the form of interviews, conversations and discussions, for all of which the creation and use of relationships is fundamental. These working relationships have certain characteristics that differentiate them from family, neighbourly or friendship ties, although as will be seen there are also many similarities. They are generally of a temporary nature, they are directed towards fulfilling the needs of the client and not those of the social worker (though his own needs may also be met indirectly and this is discussed below), they have objectives other than mutual satisfaction and enjoyment and the social worker plays the role of an outside party who is not *directly* involved in the situation, though the degree of involvement may increase over the course of time in specific cases where relationships become intense. These characteristics, it should be noted, apply with equal force to environmental strategies in which the social worker uses relationships with others in work on behalf of his clients.

A further difference between relationships that arise ordinarily in the course of life and those that are created by the intervention of a social worker lies in the starting point of the latter. Relationships between social workers and clients are established because of the presence of some need or problem which is interfering with satisfactory social functioning. The relationship becomes effective when the client perceives that there is something to be gained from it and this requires certain kinds of response from the social worker in terms of offering help and perhaps solutions. Conversely, the relationship fails to become effective if the client is unable to perceive that it can be of any use to him and he will therefore tend to withdraw from the situation if free to do so, or limit his involvement if compelled by some legal requirement to remain in contact with the social worker. These statements may make the creation of social work relationships seem like a mechanical process, a stimulus-response exercise in which human warmth is notably absent, in stark contrast to friendships that arise spontaneously and are free to develop without formal constraints. In spite of the importance of control in social work relationships, for some clients they nevertheless develop reality and significance on a level that is comparable with the most important family and friendship bonds of life and to explain this it is necessary to examine social work relationships more deeply.

On the part of the client, there may be needs beyond those immediately apparent, as was indicated in the discussion of presenting and underlying problems in Chapter 3. These needs may include a yearning for satisfactory and satisfying human relationships, or a desire to explore different ways of relating with others. These are needs that can sometimes be met in social work and if suitably handled it may eventually become possible for the client to use the experience in other contexts, thus establishing a more rewarding life pattern independently of the social worker. Whether or not these fundamental human needs exist, the social worker also contributes to the relationship something of himself and this is apparent even in the most superficial and fleeting of contacts. Any relationship is a two-way process which needs nurturing and maintaining. The exchanges that take place in relationships between social workers and clients are different in kind, since it is the social functioning of the client and not of the social worker that is the focus of attention, but the differences in quality are usually less apparent. What is important is that the contributions of each should be relevant to the work being done.

The social worker's contribution to the relationship with the client springs basically from his concern for other human beings and especially for those in obvious need or trouble. This is not a quality that can be put on to fit the occasion like a suit of clothes, but rather a key characteristic of the personality of the social worker. His concern for others should be obvious to all who meet him because it is demonstrated by his behaviour. In relation to clients it is expressed in courteous language, kindness, serious interest in them and their difficulties, and the creation of an atmosphere of confidentiality that inspires confidence and trust. This means that the social worker must be a real person, not a mechanical robot. Although some of these qualities are innate rather than acquired, they can be developed and refined to the point where their use becomes a highly skilled operation, which is nevertheless an integrated part of the personality of the social worker. This is a difficult point to grasp unless it is seen as part of the process of personality development that is common to all mankind, in which already existing attributes are enhanced and others added through experience that is at first self-conscious but later becomes what is sometimes called 'second nature'. In this sense, it is not unlike the experience of learning to drive a car in which self-consciousness and mistakes are eventually succeeded by spontaneity and expertise.

This somewhat idealistic conception of the social worker must be countered by the reality that members of the profession are no less human than other men and women and have to contend with aspects of their own personalities that are dysfunctional in their work. Motivation for social work as a career is a complex matter, but generally a mixture of altruistic and selfish elements is involved. Among the latter are the wish to exercise power over the lives of others, curiosity about the more intimate aspects of human behaviour, and a desire for satisfaction from relationships which can be controlled. These are a few general illustrations of what is highly complex and individualised, but the recognition that social workers are subject to the pressure of baser motives is the reason for emphasising in their training the importance of self-awareness, so that they may learn to control those aspects of their personalities that are likely to interfere with the satisfactory performance of their work. This is part of what being a professional means: the ability to subjugate personal interests to the needs of others. On the positive side, social workers are motivated by that love of their fellow human beings that is the true meaning of charity. The use of the word 'love' in the context of social work may lead to misunderstanding and confusion, because it is a term that has become debased and is now associated primarily with sexual attachment; but in the sense of a disposition to think favourably of others and a desire to do them good, its meaning holds true. Nor is it improper to admit that social workers often come to regard their clients with affection and that this can be a mutual feeling without exceeding the boundaries of a professional relationship. Indeed, care and concern for another implies an element of affection, which can sometimes act as a catalyst in producing change for the better.

A further question is whether it is necessary for social workers to like their clients as well as to love them. The answer to this is obvious if liking is associated with approval. At times, it may be possible for social workers to regard their clients with approval, but this is not always the case. The behaviour of some clients may provoke strong negative feelings on the part of the social worker, such as anger and revulsion, especially in situations where neglect or cruelty are involved. These are personal reactions which any human being can experience, not least a social worker, but in the context of a professional relationship they have to be put on one side insofar as is possible. This may be difficult, but awareness and understanding of one's own strongly negative feelings provide a basis for controlling their expression. Strongly positive feelings towards the client may equally blind the social worker to the real issues and inhibit his capacity to be helpful. To sum up, the social worker attempts to understand his own feelings about clients, trying to bring them into perspective and control their expression so that they are used helpfully, whether or not he has a personal liking for the individual concerned and approves of his behaviour; but throughout his work he tries to express that love for others that is represented more by attitudes than by feelings and which he shows impartially to all.

Phases in Social Work Relationships

In Chapters 3 and 4 of this book, social work is described as a process involving a sequence of stages and this is a model that is equally applicable to the analysis of social work relationships. These can be said to pass through three principal phases: initiation; maintenance and development; and termination and transfer.

Initiation. For most clients, a first meeting with a social worker is an unaccustomed experience which they tend to associate with other unpleasant aspects of life, such as going to the doctor or reporting to the headmaster's study. This is inevitable in that human beings, in Britain anyway, take great pride in being able to manage their affairs without help from outsiders beyond family and friends, so that approaching a social worker for help is often seen as a major and regrettable step. It is even worse when the social worker is thrust upon the client by virtue of the latter's delinquent or otherwise aberrant behaviour. Similar reactions may also be apparent when a community worker makes initial approaches to residents on an estate, who may well regard him with a mixture of reserve and suspicion until his intervention provides evidence to the contrary. In such situations, first impressions are of great importance and a false step at this stage can produce difficulties that may be very hard to surmount later.

The social worker has to overcome the limitations of being seen as an official, a label that may be attached to him by clients whatever his employing agency, statutory or voluntary. He must be able to convince clients that although he is a paid professional, he is concerned to identify problems and provide appropriate help, for which he may have resources or access to resources that are relevant. He should therefore aim to present himself as an approachable, receptive person, who has the patience to listen to others. He must also be prepared to make his own verbal contributions not only to give direct help, but also to convey to clients the kind of person he is, thus providing the basis from which a relationship can develop. Every small detail may be significant, including manner of speech, use of language, style of dress, visual responses and gestures. If the meeting takes place in the social worker's office, the reception accorded to the client on entering the building, the surroundings in which the interview takes place and the degree of respect accorded to the client are all of crucial importance. Similarly, in visiting a home or in meeting clients in a public building such as a community centre, the behaviour of the social worker on first contact transmits messages to the client at both conscious and unconscious levels. The client's interpretation of the social worker's behaviour is the basis on which he assesses whether there is anything to be gained from allowing a relationship to develop.

The actual behaviour of the social worker is affected not only by personal preferences but also by factors such as agency policy and professional conventions, which may influence matters like style of dress or the way a meeting is conducted. Even so, each social worker acquires his own characteristic ways of establishing contact with clients, so there is no prescription which can be provided to suit all. An awareness of the factors that have been mentioned must be coupled with a sensitive understanding of the ways in which the social worker may use his own personality traits to good effect. It is relevant to note at this point that in order to create a good working relationship it may be necessary for early meetings between social worker and client to contain much apparently 'non-relevant' material. Included under this heading are such aspects as discussion of the weather and admiring the flowers in the garden. Although these may seem purposeless, they and other apparently unrelated aspects provide means by which clients begin to assess whether the social worker is a person they wish to know and trust. Such areas of discussion often form part of ongoing work and achieve a kind of symbolic significance that demonstrates a caring attitude. Similarly, shared activities, such as drinking tea, may also symbolise the sharing of problems. The caveat to this is that fringe activities may obscure the true purpose of the meeting. This may be in accordance with the wishes of the client, at any rate in part, as he may prefer to avoid attending to painful matters by turning the meeting into a social occasion. On the other hand, the social worker who over-emphasises social pleasantries may cause confusion on the part of the client because the true purpose of the meeting is not mentioned or clarified. There should thus be a balance between the two elements, but no social worker should think it unprofessional to drink tea or play with the children, while carrying on a conversation with the client that is relevant to his reasons for intervention.

A further point is connected with the expectations of the social worker. By the very nature of the work, he becomes accustomed to forming good working relationships quickly and may forget that for some clients this is a novel experience in which they can move only slowly and tentatively. Although a quick and ready response may sometimes by elicited at a first meeting between social worker and client, the process of forming a relationship often takes much longer. In some cases it can even be spread over a period of years, particularly if the client concerned has hitherto had mainly destructive experiences of human relationships. In some extreme cases, it may seem impossible to create a relationship, however much the social worker perseveres. Whatever the situation, it is vital for the social worker to be patient and to follow one of the central principles of social work, going at the client's pace. This needs emphasis, because it is so easy for the social worker to impose his own expectations of behaviour on the client without realising that he is doing it and to make demands for responses or changes that are unrealistic at a particular stage of the relationship.

Finally, it is not always realistic for social workers to expect the kind of responses that indicate that their offer of a relationship is welcome. Some clients are unable to indicate much of a response by reason of handicap or disease. Examples of this are some of those who are mentally retarded, deaf, mentally disordered or suffering from senile deterioration. Others may display a response of indifference or hostility, particularly if the intervention of the social worker is imposed on them by legal process. Probation and supervision orders do not generally require the client concerned to form a relationship with a social worker, though many choose to do so. In these and other similar situations, the social worker may have the feeling of working in the dark, acting according to what he understands and believes to be best for the client, but doing so in the absence of direct feedback, except in the form of observable behaviour which may be misleading or capable of different interpretations. The capacity to persevere in the face of uncertainty and to use imaginatively whatever opportunities present themselves is another aspect of skill in social work. Imaginative understanding is especially important in the early stages of a relationship, since it carries conviction of the desire of the social worker to provide positive help and creates the belief that this is possible.

Maintenance and Development. It has already been suggested elsewhere in this book that much social work involves isolated or short-term contacts with clients and some further aspects of this, related to intervention in crisis situations, are discussed in the final section of this chapter. Short-term contacts require all of the skills discussed under the heading of relationships and they need them to be developed to a high level in which the single interview, visit or meeting can be used to achieve maximum effectiveness. Nevertheless, there are many situations in which because of the needs of the client or the requirements of society, or both together, the social worker's involvement in a case is of a longer duration. Long-term work can range from six to a dozen meetings to contact over a period of years, depending on the nature of the problems involved. Thus worker and client may agree to meet regularly for a limited period to work on specific problems, as in task-centred work. In contrast, children in local authority care are the concern of the social worker for as long as they remain in care, which may be many years. When such long-term contact is maintained it is common for there to be many changes of social worker and although this gives children the opportunity to build relationships with a succession of adults, it has the disadvantage of conveying to them that few relationships are enduring and this can have damaging effects on their later experiences in marriage and as parents themselves. If such changes of relationship in long-term work are to be made as beneficial as possible it is essential that transferring the child to a new social worker should be handled sensitively and effectively, along the lines discussed in the next section of this chapter. Irrespective of whether the social worker expects his involvement in a situation to last for years rather than months or weeks and also of whether the contact is terminable only by factors outside his control (such as the age of the client) or by mutual negotiation and agreement, the ability to maintain and develop relationships in a purposeful manner is an essential social work skill. Relationships develop as social workers and clients work together on the problems or circumstances that have become the focus for concern and they are nurtured and made effective in two ways: through understanding and through the skilled use of appropriate strategies of intervention.

As knowledge about the client and his situation increases, so should the social worker's understanding of its relevance and importance develop. This is in part the process of assessment that is discussed at length in Chapter 3 and which continues throughout the duration of a case. Understanding is developed in the context of meetings between social worker and client but should be enhanced by thought and study and by the writing of records, as means of assisting the social worker to clarify his ideas and hypotheses. It is important for social workers to spend time analysing what clients tell them, linking points together, assessing their significance and restructuring the material into new patterns, which are then tested in further discussion with the people concerned. It is relevant here to refer to Leighton's concept of the 'act of understanding' mentioned in Chapter 3.[1] However much the social worker analyses the material he gains from interaction with the client, it is in the dynamic interchange that takes place between them that real understanding emerges, because it is subjective and not objective reality that is important. Since subjective reality is prone to change, the social worker must approach each meeting with the client as a fresh encounter in which both may modify views and attitudes as understanding changes and develops.

As understanding grows, the relevance of specific strategies of intervention becomes clearer and the social worker is able to select and apply these as circumstances require. In the application of strategies there is inevitably a great deal of trial and error, since human differences make for uncertainty of outcome and in any case the social worker is never in possession of complete understanding of a situation. Nevertheless, understanding often supplies sufficient clues about which strategies may be appropriate and which to avoid. This may be supplemented by inviting the participation of the client in the choice of strategies, so that social work intervention becomes a shared activity. Thus, a community worker may invite a group to decide with him on the most appropriate method of solving their difficulties, perhaps choosing between self-help activities that involve the social worker in creating opportunities and social action that involves drawing the attention of others to their plight. Similarly, a social worker engaged in some of the influencing strategies may actively seek the co-operation of the client in a programme of behaviour modification, for which a positive relationship is an essential foundation.

The use of the word 'relationship' implies the development of a strong bond between people and this in itself is often the source of much help for the client. The feeling that someone else, albeit a professional person, has confidence and faith in his ability to solve his own problems successfully is often an incentive to do so. Alternatively, the client may come to feel that he has made a kind of bargain with the social worker, which demands that they both fulfil obligations. As the relationship develops, there are certain aspects of which the social worker needs to be aware if he is to maintain an element of objectivity in his approach and use his skills in the most positive way possible. Three such aspects require special consideration in this context: transference, dependence and ambivalence.

Transference is a technical term originating from psychoanalysis, where it is used as the core of treatment involving the elucidation and clarification of feelings towards significant others, particularly parental figures. These feelings, often largely unconscious in origin, are played out in the context of the relationship with the analyst. In social work, the term 'transference' is used in a broader sense to describe those feelings which human beings tend to transfer from one relationship to another, however appropriately or inappropriately. Thus many social workers are authority figures and are seen by clients in terms of their previous experience of such persons, for example father, teacher or policeman. Sometimes this means that all authority figures are seen as punitive, whereas the social worker is trying to provide experience of the benevolent aspects of authority. This he does partly through actions and behaviour in general, but it may also be necessary to discuss with the client his previous experiences of authority and assist him towards a different, more positive view. It must be emphasised that social workers are concerned with attitudes to authority as they affect current behaviour. It is not appropriate for them to ape the analyst by investigating the unconscious levels of personality. Nevertheless, in any person's life, a great deal of past experience may be found in present behaviour and attitudes and this can provide fruitful material for discussion. The counterpart of transference, known as counter-transference, is also of relevance to the social worker, insofar as it is concerned with the feelings which the client evokes in the worker. These need to be identified and understood if the worker is to maintain a professional approach and avoid the dangers of over-involvement, which clouds judgement and reduces the capacity to help by placing on the client inappropriate demands for gratification. Properly understood and controlled, the feelings that the social worker develops towards the client provide a further dimension to understanding.

The playing of specific roles is closely related to transference and often provides a useful means of developing a relationship. The assumption of a variety of roles and the ability to move from one to another are social skills necessary for all human beings. Thus adults are husbands and wives, the children of their own parents and the parents of their own children, in addition to carrying a variety of work and leisure roles. The extent of satisfactory and appropriate performance in roles is an important element in the social worker's assessment of the client as well as contributing to his general understanding of individuals and groups. Furthermore, all human beings are involved in complex role relationships, deficiencies in the performance of any of which may produce damaging effects. As a result, social workers sometimes find it necessary and appropriate to adopt substitute roles in regard to clients, for example paternal or maternal roles towards children and adolescents. This kind of parenting may be of value if it is reality-based and consciously designed to counteract or make good earlier damaging experience. It is also important that it should not merely be used as an escape from other problems in the client's life. Thus it would be purely self-indulgent for worker and client to engage in a satisfying parent-child relationship, if this was being used to avoid other aspects of a disruptive home life, though it might provide an appropriate starting point for work on a wider basis, particularly if the eventual aim was to effect improvements in the client's relationship with his own parents. It is usually important, therefore, that the assumption of roles should be limited in duration, except in such situations as residential child care and fostering, in which the nature of the work requires staff to act in a parental capacity, often for substantial periods of time. Even in those circumstances, however, it is important to avoid delusions about the true nature of the situation. The workers concerned do not become parents, but act as professionals in parental roles, usually on a 'caretaking' basis. In residential situations where groups of clients are involved, there are also many opportunities for individuals to experiment in the assumption of different roles under expert guidance, both in play (as when children play 'mothers and fathers') and in performing tasks that require organisation, such as an expedition to the countryside. Such role playing is also of general relevance to work with groups. In community groups, it is often necessary to create formal roles, such as chairman and treasurer, but it may not be possible for local people to take on these responsibilities until they have witnessed a demonstration from the social worker of what is involved. In more formal group work, role playing exercises may be used to enable members to free themselves of inhibitions and develop new capacities in a structured situation.

Dependence is closely related to roles and is an unavoidable feature of continuing social work relationships, largely because of the unequal basis of helper and helped on which these are founded. Dependence, used in this context to mean emotional dependence, implies leaning on someone and is characteristic of all life's relationships, since few people ever reach a state of complete independence. The concept of social functioning implies the acquisition of sufficient independence to act as a responsible adult, relating to others on a mature level for most of the time, with the capacity to take decisions effectively. It is perhaps an unattainable ideal for many people, but their capacity for independence can often be enhanced through relationships with others, particularly with those like social workers who set out to promote self-responsibility. The road to independent functioning often lies through a period of dependence in which the client can sort out and reorganise himself, supported by a warm and satisfying relationship with someone who has become important in his life. It is easy to encourage dependence in clients without realising that it is happening. The solution of problems may often appear more easily achievable if the social worker acts unilaterally, but the price paid may be increased dependence and an expectation on the client's part that subsequent difficulties will be similarly resolved, thus reducing motivation for self-responsibility. This problem poses a considerable dilemma for those who work with community groups. If the worker is active in seeking solutions himself, the eventual result may be apathy and dissolution of the group when he leaves. On the other hand, if the worker tries to be non-directive and encourage independent thinking, little may be achieved and the group will fail to develop its own problem-solving skills. Dependence thus needs to be carefully controlled if it is to be used in the client's interest. It should be fostered where it is likely to contribute to personal growth but discouraged if it produces inertia.

Some members of society are inescapably faced with continuing dependence, whether emotional or physical, by reason of suffering from some handicap or personal inadequacy which cannot be remedied. However willing they are to accept their condition, they are no less likely than anyone else to experience a mixture of feelings about it. Such mixed feelings are known as *ambivalence* and this is a prevalent characteristic of social work relationships for the obvious reason that although clients often need what the social worker has to offer, they frequently feel resentful at having to ask for it, since this is an admission of their own inadequacy. Ambivalence also permeates most relationships in life and is therefore a central element in social work assessment and intervention. It is of relevance to the client's relationships with family, friends, employers and so on, and also to behaviour within groups and community organisations. The social worker must be adept at dealing with both the positive and the negative aspects of ambivalence. In general, it is easier to cope with positive feelings, which cause little discomfort, but it must be noted that these are often exaggerated in order to hide stronger negative emotions. The social worker must carefully evaluate the strength of positive feelings and when he judges them to be excessive must attempt to enable the client to express the negative and perhaps painful emotions that may also be present. This is necessary if the full implications of the client's problems are to be understood and tackled and includes the negative feelings of the client towards the social worker, such as frustration and anger at not being helped effectively. At times this may go as far as encouraging the expression of open hostility, either from individuals or in groups and although this is never easy to face because of its potentially unpleasant and unwelcome consequences, it has to be accepted as a normal and natural component of human emotions that cannot be ignored in problem-solving. In working with a community group, it may be particularly important to bring mutual hostilities out into the open as a means of resolving difficulties that are inhibiting the achievement of the group's objectives.

As his confidence in the social worker grows, the client may begin to reveal more about himself, which may add to and even alter the picture of problems and needs so far established. At times, he may feel that he has revealed too much and experience guilt at what he has told the social worker about his feelings towards others among his family or friends. The social worker can help by conveying to the client that it is common for the relief experienced by sharing difficulties to be accompanied by reservations about the extent to which normally closely guarded feelings should be brought out into the open, and this provides reassurance to the client in dealing with this kind of ambivalence. At other times, emotional outpourings are followed by fallow periods in which little seems to be happening and the social worker may wonder whether to terminate his involvement. It is important to remember that all relationships have such phases, moving from intense activity and involvement to withdrawal and contemplation. The social worker should be prepared for this and not rush into withdrawal himself, until he is sure that the objectives of intervention have been achieved or no further progress can be made for the time being.

Termination and Transfer. The cessation of relationships that have achieved emotional significance for those involved is inevitably accompanied by a mixture of reactions, another aspect of ambivalence. Such reactions are perhaps observed most clearly in those who are grieving for a loved one lost through death but they are also present in other life situations involving a dramatic break, such as dismissal from employment or the end of a love affair. In social work, when the relationship has developed significance for the client, similar reactions of grief and mourning are sometimes apparent when the point of termination is near. Although the intensity of involvement is not usually as great as in a deep personal relationship, it is nevertheless necessary for the social worker to be able to deal with feelings that are evoked by the prospect of termination, both his own and those of the client.

Social work relationships may come to an end in any of three ways: they may be terminated by the client, or by the social worker, or they may be transferred, as when the social worker hands over responsibility to a colleague. From the point of view of the social worker, termination by the client is probably the most unsatisfactory way in which to complete a piece of work. In its most negative aspects, it takes the form of failure of the client to keep an appointment or refusal to admit the social worker into the home and unless there are statutory regulations which require continued contact, it must usually be accepted that the end has been reached. In such situations, it is important for social workers to examine what has happened in previous contact with the client, to discover if there are any clues to indicate why the relationship has been terminated. It may be that in seeking to provide effective help, the social worker has raised in discussion aspects of the client's life or behaviour which are too painful for him to consider and he has therefore 'run away'. Another possibility is that he has found the help offered by the social worker of no use or apparent relevance to his problems, or that he has solved his difficulties in other ways. It is not always possible for social workers to find ways of offering effective help, particularly when clients come seeking the impossible, such as the instantaneous solution of their interpersonal problems. Such clients may persevere for a while, but give up when they realise that the social worker does not possess the powers they imagined and expected. In contrast, it sometimes happens that the client terminates the relationship simply because he has been helped effectively and therefore no longer requires assistance. It is difficult to produce evidence for this, for the obvious reason that the social worker usually has no opportunity to discuss the outcome with the client, but in cases in which strategies such as the release of feelings or the provision of material aid have been predominant, experience suggests that the help received may be sufficient to meet the needs of the client and restore social functioning.

Termination by the client corresponds to haphazard termination as discussed in Chapter 4. Preordained and planned termination provide the social worker with opportunities to bring work to a more satisfactory close, either permanently or as a prelude to transfer. To carry out the procedure of terminating a case effectively, the social worker must pay attention to three specific aspects. First, consideration must be given to the correct timing, which ideally should be the point at which the client is ready to manage unaided, an adequate level of social functioning having been achieved. This is a matter of judgement and the development of skill in assessment through experience. It is rarely a clear-cut question and there are often risks involved, as when an offender is released from the conditions of a probation order before its normal date of expiry. Inexperienced social workers are likely to be over-cautious about termination, though some go to the opposite extreme and appear hasty and even reckless in this matter, so it is important that they should have opportunities for consultation with experienced senior staff, an aspect of practice that is discussed in Chapter 12.

The second consideration for the social worker thinking of terminating a case is that adequate preparation should be given to the client or group concerned. It is usually advisable to reduce the frequency of meetings as soon as the possibility of termination becomes apparent. The prospect of termination should also be discussed with the client well in advance of its possibility, allowing a month or two for adjusting to the idea and accepting it. The client should be encouraged to discuss his feelings about the prospect, both positive and negative, so that by the time the break takes place, he has reconciled opposing views within himself and achieved some stability of outlook for the future. This is a good time to look back over what has happened to the client in the course of his relationship with the social worker, highlighting positive achievements and emphasising any gains that the client has made in his social functioning. It is also wise to discuss with the client aspects of the future and the ways in which he may be able to cope with new problems on his own. It is sometimes helpful to offer the possibility of a renewal of the relationship should circumstances demand it, or to indicate that the agency employing the social worker will be able to offer help in the future if needed.

The third consideration is the desirability that as far as possible the decision to terminate the relationship should be one arrived at by mutual agreement between the parties concerned. Sometimes it is possible to start the relationship on this basis, as when a social worker agrees with an individual or group to meet for a fixed number of sessions, after which their contact will be terminated. This arrangement has many advantages in cases in which problems and needs are clear and may act as an incentive to the clients involved to elucidate their troubles more quickly because of the limited time available. In other cases, however, the real problems and needs do not emerge until after a period of uncertainty and confusion has been experienced, so that the timing of termination has to be settled at a later stage in the development of the relationship. Even so, mutual agreement between client and worker is likely to produce a more positive outcome than a decision taken unilaterally by the social worker, which risks evoking excessive resentment and hostility. It should be noted that even when termination occurs by mutual agreement, it is still important to provide preparation during the weeks preceding the event itself.

Adequate preparation is also necessary in cases where responsibility is being transferred to another worker. The client must be told soon enough to have time to discuss his feelings about the prospect and to withdraw some of his involvement with the present worker in anticipation of starting a new relationship with his successor. When possible, it is helpful for the client to be introduced to the new worker by his present social worker. It is also important for the client to be clear about how much the new worker will be told about him in advance, as this can reduce the burden of feeling that one has to start 'all over again'. Transfer is a very common experience for people who are longer-term clients of social work agencies, either because of changes of staff or because of their own mobility which takes them into new geographical areas that are covered by different departments. Although such breaks in relationship are often deplored, they also have positive aspects, particularly for clients who are learning about relationships through their contact with social workers. Changes of worker provide such clients with opportunities to demonstrate increasing ability in forming relationships which can enhance their social functioning in general.

Crisis Intervention and Short-Term Work

Social work intervention is most commonly a response to an emotional or situational crisis, manifested in such varied experiences as a court appearance, eviction from home, mental or physical illness, or, on a larger scale, problems related to the cleanliness of an estate or redevelopment plans. At one time, social workers took the view that few problems were capable of speedy solution and accordingly favoured long-term work as the most effective means of providing help. This attitude has come under attack in recent years, partly because pressures of demand for the services of social workers have been so great that long-term work has become a luxury, but also because research findings have led to the conclusion that shorter-term work may be more effective in some cases.

When short-term work is contemplated or has become the norm, it is particularly important that intervention should take place at the point of crisis. Writers such as Caplan[2] and Rapoport[3] have suggested that under the stress of a crisis, individuals and families are more open to receiving help than at other times, and that assistance that enables them to surmount their difficulties successfully constitutes a good investment for the future, in that there is then a better chance that such people will be able to deal with further troubles without calling on professional advice. Moreover, it is the quality rather than the quantity of help that is important. 'A little help, rationally directed and purposefully focused at a strategic time is more effective than more extensive help given at a period of less emotional accessibility.'[4] Rapoport goes on to argue that the 'helping person needs to view himself as intervening in a social system—as part of a network of relationships—and not as a single resource',[5] giving support to the view that in crisis intervention it is often necessary to involve many other professional workers on a multi-disciplinary basis. These other workers include doctors, nurses, home helps and other workers with relevant knowledge and skills. It is also important to emphasise the need for speedy attention to the problems manifested. The duration of a crisis is rarely more than a few weeks, since there is a natural human tendency to adjust and adapt, and once this point is reached, the opportunity for effective intervention is likely to be lost, however precarious the new state of equilibrium.

These findings are significant both for the strategies and for the skills employed by social workers. The former must be brought into play speedily, perhaps in situations in which social workers have hitherto concentrated on other aspects of their role, such as pre-trial enquiries for the courts, which have often been regarded as information-gathering exercises rather than as opportunities to provide help in a crisis. Although this may produce some role confusion for social workers, there is ample evidence from experience that the most effective work with offenders is often carried out immediately before and after the court appearance and this is entirely in accordance with crisis theory. A further implication is the extension of social work intervention into areas as yet barely touched upon, including the needs of many hospital patients with acute illnesses who do not receive social work help and of prisoners on remand, for whom the prison welfare service is beginning to provide assistance at some penal institutions. It is also vitally important that social workers should become aware of crisis situations early enough for their intervention to achieve maximum effect. Many of the problems which social workers tackle are the result of months or even years of troubles, which may be known to relatives or other agencies, such as schools or hospitals, but which have not been referred to social workers until the prospects of successful solution seem hopeless. Much valuable preventive work would be possible if social workers became involved when the difficulties first arose.

As far as the skills of social workers are concerned, crisis intervention demands the capacity to be selective in terms of focus and consequently the ability to leave unexplored related or underlying problems that may not be immediately relevant, or for tackling which there is insufficient time. Some writers, including Irvine, consider that this type of skill is highly advanced: 'We have a lot to learn about short-term focused work, the skill of helping the client just enough to restore or achieve adequate functioning in respect of the problem presented without opening up his problems in general and becoming sunk for years in the effort to resolve them. This I would regard as very advanced indeed.'[6] Nevertheless, the demands of the job now require most social workers to be skilled in crisis work and short-term intervention.

10

Relationships in Social Work

(ii) *Clients and the Environment*

In the course of a day's activities, social workers find themselves engaged in a varied and complex pattern of relationships, which demand the capacity to adapt quickly from one situation to another. At one moment they may be concentrating on a one-to-one interview in the privacy of an office, immediately after which they may be required, in stark contrast, to give what is nothing less than a public performance, such as speaking in court or at a meeting of a community association. Effective social work practice demands the capacity to make such rapid changes of orientation without loss of concentration, although there are often opportunities, such as a car journey or refreshment break, in which to prepare oneself for the next task. In Chapter 5, it was indicated that the social worker has to make decisions about the dimensions of his work, which involve choices about working with individuals, pairs, families, groups and the environment. Although the strategies of social intervention discussed in Chapters 6 to 8 are relevant to all five dimensions, each of these dimensions has special characteristics in terms of relationships, which in turn influence the choice of strategies in each case.

Individuals

One of the great strengths of social work lies in its ability to respond to people as individuals rather than as members of categories. Social workers and the literature of social work lay great emphasis on the importance of individual differences and the consequent need for differential treatment that is specially adapted to the needs of each client. The ability to focus on the individual as such is a vital contributory factor in the establishment of what is sometimes described as 'rapport', the emotional bond from which a relationship grows. It is also related to another term which is used in connection with social work relationships, 'empathy', by which is meant the power to feel imaginatively the experiences of another person. At a more mundane level, this might be described as being able to 'get on the same wavelength' as the client, providing a true basis for mutual understanding. Thus although it is rarely possible for the social worker to experience himself the feelings of the client in all their intensity and confusion, he may come near to it in imaginative terms and it is this ability to 'put oneself in another person's shoes' that is the hallmark of a skilled and empathetic professional. It should be noted here that the social worker is concerned with empathy rather than with sympathy. The former involves the use of the imagination and of one's own feelings as a guide to understanding, assessment and intervention. The latter implies complete loss of objectivity and the involvement of one's own feelings with those of the client to an extent where the capacity to take a detached view is compromised by personal considerations. Sympathy in these terms is not an appropriate part of professional practice, though few would deny that social workers need a compassionate approach to human problems.

The most important justification for any specific form of relationship treatment in social work is that it meets the needs of the client. On this basis, a case can be made out for all the dimensions outlined in the model of social work intervention described in Chapter 5. The individual, however, has established a special place in social work practice and it is in this area that most has been learned about the nature of the task and the skills involved. One important contributory factor has undoubtedly been the influence of psychoanalytic theories on social work practice, which led workers to adopt a therapist-patient treatment model, often to the extent of excluding work in other dimensions. Another influence has probably been the relative comfort experienced in a one-to-one relationship. It may be both intimate and personally satisfying, as well as relatively easy for the social worker to control and limit, in contrast to situations in which several clients are dealt with at the same time. It can also be argued that working with individuals has played a special part in meeting social workers' own needs for rewarding relationships, particularly when it has been possible to work on a long-term basis with frequent contact between worker and client. Although these influences have at times led to an unduly narrow approach to social work intervention and may even have produced inappropriate choices of dimension in relation to specific problems, they also reflect the needs of many, although not perhaps all clients.

Early in the development of social work, it was recognised that people need their individuality and the opportunity to express it. Many clients live in circumstances in which for much of the time they are denied individuality, whether in the home or at work or during their leisure time, in any of which situations they may be no more than one of a crowd. Some would argue that this problem has increased in intensity as society has become more complex and impersonal. Thus it is suggested that the consequences of urbanisation and technological change leave little scope for individual expression, except perhaps in deviant forms such as delinquent behaviour or mental breakdown. These are two of the many similar reasons why people become the clients of social workers. Social workers' clients are usually undergoing some kind of stress and for many such people recognition that they are individuals who matter in their own right provides them with an incentive to set about restoring their social functioning to an adequate level. This is further enhanced by the fact that the social worker is also an individual, though different from those they meet in daily social intercourse, in that he stands outside their situation and is not directly involved in it and also in that he makes no direct demands on them to gratify his own needs. The needs of individuals are particularly important in residential care. The effects of institutionalisation and mass living are well known in terms of their detrimental effect on individual functioning and it is therefore of vital importance that people living in residential centres should be given individual care and treatment, as well as the opportunity to participate in group activities.

Dealing with clients as individuals demands considerable powers of concentration on the part of the social worker, if needs are to be met effectively. He must be able to exclude from his mind all thoughts about his other responsibilities and activities, including those which are noted next in his diary, for it is vital for the client to feel that for the moment he and his troubles are all that matter. This skill is an asset to the social worker in all of his activities, whenever he is in conversation with an individual, be it client, colleague, official or member of the community. It is also of importance whether or not the solution to the client's difficulties lies within the one-to-one relationship or extends beyond it to work with other people and in the environment.

It is sometimes relevant to interpret the existence of individual and family problems as products of the structure of society, a view which is undeniably valid in considering such phenomena as poverty, unemployment and inequality in general. In these circumstances, it may rightly be suggested that social work with individuals is of little relevance and may even be dysfunctional insofar as it strives to make people more contented with the injustices which afflict them. For some people, however, there are problems which are less related to these factors than to their own relationship with society and their attitudes and feelings about their very existence. These are the people for whom individual help is often essential, because it provides them with an opportunity to think through their difficulties in the presence of an interested listener whose effectiveness may lie more in asking the right questions than in providing solutions. Such people may need to examine the pattern of their life so far, in order to understand and perhaps come to terms with it before venturing in new directions. They may need to discover new ways of dealing with their feelings and their reactions to some of life's events such as bereavement, disability or the prospect of retirement. Finally, they may need to talk through their own chaotic relationships in an attempt to learn new ways of behaving that will evoke from others more positive responses that will in turn increase personal satisfaction. The social worker can help the client to find his own solutions by listening to the difficulties, making sense of them, questioning and prompting sensitively and offering choices between realistic alternatives.

For people whose problems are thus 'inside' them in some way, individual help may well be the most effective method of intervention, though this should not exclude the possibility of treatment in a group, should the circumstances suggest it and the client be willing. As with all approaches, it is helpful to discuss the possibilities fully with the client and offer alternatives if available. The question of individual or group treatment has particular relevance in dealing with social isolates, those clients who appear to be disconnected from family and friendship ties and who have few, if any, meaningful relationships in their lives. A case can be made out for individual treatment, in the hope that through developing a close relationship with the social worker they will find a model for creating close ties with others they meet. On the other hand, the demands of an individual relationship may be so great that they can only respond by withdrawing further into isolation. In that case they may be more appropriately dealt with in a group, in which they can 'lose' themselves to some extent and have greater freedom of choice about the ties they develop. Relationships in and with groups are discussed in a subsequent section of this chapter. In the present context, it is emphasised that, where appropriate, social work that offers an individual relationship is a legitimate and necessary part of practice. Furthermore, it is the point at which a great deal of social work intervention begins and is therefore an essential area of skill for all practitioners.

Pairs

The desire for a deeply personal and mutually satisfying relationship with one other person is most obviously demonstrated in western society by the marriage bond and the rituals and conventions which surround it, but it is also to be observed in varying intensity in other ties, such as those between brother and sister and between friends. In social work, the relationship between two people most commonly expresses itself in a form requiring help when marital troubles occur, but there are also workers who are concerned with the preparation of engaged couples for marriage and on occasions the problems of two warring elderly relatives sharing accommodation are manifested in ways that lead to intervention. Thus, although most of the literature concerned with pairs deals with the marital relationship, it is by no means irrelevant to other situations in which two people are experiencing difficulties in an intense and dependent relationship.

One of the first considerations in dealing with a problem that involves two people is the question of whether each is in need of individual attention rather than shared help in a three-cornered relationship with the social worker. Some husbands and wives are so embroiled in their own individual problems that they cannot begin to consider those of their partner and the relationship between them, until they have experienced help in a one-to-one situation and that is the form in which a great deal of marital work takes place. In some specialist agencies, such as the Institute of Marital Studies in London, it is the practice to assign a separate worker to each partner. This has also been tried elsewhere, notably in some of the marital work carried out by the probation and after-care service, and has been found to work well. It has the advantage of providing each partner with individual attention while avoiding the difficulties of sharing that are often fundamental to their disordered relationship. It is also possible for one social worker to deal with both partners separately without any necessary loss of effectiveness, although it requires considerable skill in handling issues of equality of treatment and confidentiality. Problems of confidentiality are not absent when two workers are involved, though they may perhaps be more easily resolved. (For a discussion of confidentiality, see Chapter 11.)

One final point before turning to specific aspects of working with pairs is that although the problem is the relationship between two people, only one of them may be available to meet the social worker. This may arise for several reasons: the partner who has sought help may not wish the other party to be informed or involved; the other party may refuse to be seen or alternatively be inaccessible by reason of absence in a place unknown; or, finally, the other party may be away from home, working elsewhere or in an institution such as a psychiatric hospital or a prison, in any of which circumstances the social worker will depend on the co-operation of a colleague in another department to undertake whatever work is necessary. When it is not possible to involve the other party directly, the emphasis has to be on individual help, but that may nevertheless be of some use in influencing the relationship between the pair insofar as it helps the one to develop different and possibly more appropriate attitudes to the other. These are often observed to have beneficial reciprocal consequences and can produce a 'snowball' effect in terms of improved relationships.

When it is possible to deal with both partners as a pair, the focus moves from their functioning as individuals to the relationship that exists between them. It must be said that it is often exceptionally difficult to maintain this focus because the individual needs of each partner are also present and require attention. It is important to attempt to deal with these individual needs in the context of the pair relationship, but this may well meet resistance and hostility on the part of the clients concerned. In this context, there are often two common and complementary psychological defence mechanisms at work, the identification of which is of crucial importance in understanding the relationship and in seeking solutions to the problem. These defence mechanisms are denial and projection. Marital partners frequently display a tendency to deny individual responsibility for the difficulties they are encountering and to project the blame entirely on to the other partner. There may well be evidence that appears to justify the claims of one or other partner that the blame lies elsewhere, for example in physical cruelty or in an extra-marital relationship, but it invariably happens that such phenomena are provoked by relationship difficulties between the partners, rather than arising spontaneously in isolation. In his relationship with the pair, the social worker tries to focus on reality and on helping each partner to begin to accept some degree of responsibility for the situation and for its solution. He must also refrain from taking sides with one partner against the other, a tendency which is not entirely avoidable. Not only may he feel greater concern for one rather than for the other, but he is also prey to the desire of each individual to feel that someone is on his or her side, a reality that is easily imagined, even if the social worker has scrupulously refrained from committing himself by word or deed.

The relevance of the past has particular significance in dealing with marital problems. The expectations with which people entered marriage and their feelings about their parents and their parents' own marriages are frequently apparent even years after the event and may require discussion. Such expectations have sometimes led to distorted relationships in which perhaps the man was seeking a mother-figure for a wife or the woman looked for an authoritarian father-figure. There may also be distortions of the customary male-female roles, with the wife adopting masculine attitudes in terms of employment and control of the children and the husband playing a more feminine part in carrying out domestic activities. These examples are given to indicate that the pattern of relationships between pairs of people, particularly in marriage, is infinitely varied and not always dysfunctional, since apparent role distortions may complement the needs of both concerned. It should also be emphasised that choice of partner involves both conscious and unconscious elements. There are times when the latter come dimly into awareness and may be used in social work to help the couple to gain greater understanding of themselves and their relationships, adding to that gained by looking at the present reality of which they are only too conscious.

Social workers sometimes become involved in marital cases at a point where the needs of one partner have changed as a result of personality growth or experience elsewhere in life, such as a change of occupation, and the other is unable to adjust to a new role appropriately. In these circumstances it is necessary to explore first with the couple the prospects of achieving a new adjustment, which is sometimes possible on the lines of the reciprocal 'snowball' effect mentioned above. This is not always feasible, however, and it then becomes necessary to help the couple to find alternative solutions, perhaps accepting some emotional distance in a reformulated relationship, perhaps separating altogether. It is important to emphasise here that the social worker is not concerned with imposing his own views on the situation, nor with attempting to help the couple to attain some ideal of married bliss. His skill lies in enabling them as far as possible to find solutions in which each maintains integrity, while working towards resolving their disrupted relationship, whether by enhancing it to a level which promises some security for the future or by enabling them to make a final break satisfactorily.

Families

Social workers readily accept that many individual problems arise from and have implications for relationships within the family. This and other factors, such as an interest in promoting healthy family life, has been reflected in a range of experimental approaches, recorded in the literature under such headings as family casework and family therapy.[1] Much of this literature is derived from work in clinical situations, which attain something of an ideal in terms of commitment and co-operation on the part of the families concerned, and it is therefore of limited relevance in the British situation, where there is perhaps a greater onus on the social worker to establish effective working relationships, than in countries like the United States of America, where it appears more common for families themselves to take the initiative in seeking treatment. At this stage of development, there are no commonly accepted guidelines for social intervention with families, but the following points cover the main aspects likely to be useful in practice.

It was suggested in Chapter 8 that one way in which members of the family are of importance to the client is in their roles as 'significant others', on which account it may be relevant for the social worker to give them some attention. It was also suggested that at times members of the family may need to be treated as clients in their own right, enabling them to receive help with the problems they share with the originally identified client. In these situations, however, the social worker appears to be primarily concerned with building relationships with a number of individuals, or perhaps pairs, in order to provide help with problems that at least in origin are seen as developing from the circumstances or behaviour of one member. Thus a probation officer may be able to establish relationships with the parents of a delinquent youth and work with them as well as with their son, using whatever strategies of social intervention appear appropriate. Similarly, a social worker may give help to the members of the family of a person temporarily in hospital as a result of the onset of some mental disorder. The validity of these methods is not in question, provided they are relevant to the situation being tackled, but as they do not usually involve focusing on the social functioning of the family as a unit, they do not constitute the kind of family-centred work implied by the categorisation of the family as a dimension for social work intervention.

A truly family-centred approach in social work involves the capacity to treat the family unit as the client and to relate to it less as a set of individuals than as a group with its own particular characteristics. It means that the problems of individuals must be perceived by the social worker as aspects of the functioning of the family as a whole, in the solution of which all members share an interest. It also requires that the social worker should be able to convince the whole family that this approach is feasible and has an equal if not better chance of success than working on an individual basis with the member or members originally identified as clients. Some exponents of this approach believe that it is always necessary for the family members to be seen together if success is to be achieved. Others adopt a varied pattern, in which there are meetings with the whole family from time to time, interspersed with work with sub-groups and individuals in which the emphasis on family functioning is nevertheless retained. Provided this latter requirement can be met, the flexible approach seems to be more manageable for most British social workers, since the main means of contact with families is home visiting, in which it can be difficult to set the scene by ensuring or insisting that all members are present every time. On the other hand, in agencies which have adequate interviewing facilities it may be possible to adopt a more formal approach on North American lines, in which the family as a whole comes for regular appointments. This has been tried with success in child guidance clinics and would also be feasible in other agencies such as probation offices.

There are naturally many obstacles to the successful formation of a relationship with a family, notably the need to scapegoat the problem member by projecting on to him all blame for the difficulties the others are experiencing. This may be carried even further into denial that anyone else in the family need be concerned, since it is purely an individual problem. These views often gain endorsement from the ways in which people are referred to social workers for help, a process in which they acquire a 'problem' label which neatly categorises them and in doing so helps to absolve other family members from a sense of responsibility. Not all families behave in this way, however, although they may be encouraged to do so by the approach of the social worker who may unthinkingly collude with the individual problem label applied to the identified client, instead of seeing this as a symptom of more widespread troubles. Some families virtually ask to be treated as a unit, recognising from the start that they are all involved in the problem. Others move into wanting to become more fully involved after members have gained from the experience of being treated on an individual basis. One point that seems to be overlooked, however, is the effect that the social worker's initial approach has on the pattern of relationships established. The first meeting not only sets the tone, but also creates a structure for the future, which, with all its limitations, may become difficult to change. There is a good chance that if social workers dealt with referrals from the start as family problems and indicated that they wished to involve all members in the work to be done, many would be willing to co-operate. Some probation officers have tried this approach successfully in carrying out social enquiries for the courts, while other agencies like Family Service Units have long preferred to work on this basis.

The role of the social worker in relation to the total family unit is undoubtedly a difficult one to sustain. He must ensure that problems are elucidated and discussed in the family context, maintaining the functioning of the unit as a whole as the focus for treatment. He is likely to face bids to win his approval that would involve taking sides and becoming part of the scapegoating process. He may also be the target for a great deal of hostility and abuse, when he shows that he cannot himself take over responsibility for solving the family's problems. Although he can never become a member of the family in the literal sense, he may begin to feel that he is getting near to this as his growing knowledge and understanding of the interrelationships in the unit and between the members and himself produce in him a sense of involvement and even entanglement from which there seems to be no escape.[2] It is of the greatest importance, therefore, that social workers involved in family situations should have opportunities for consultation with senior staff about the work they are doing, in order to increase their understanding and support them in its continuance. This is all the more necessary because many of the family situations are part of a long-term pattern of disturbance and disruption. Child neglect and cruelty, homelessness and poverty are striking examples of presenting problems, with which immediate practical help may be needed. Even in those circumstances, however, the importance of working through relationships should not be ignored. Halliwell[3] has shown how in some situations of gross deprivation, it is necessary to work at building a relationship with a family before its members can begin to find strength and motivation to take action on their own behalf.

Groups

The interest of social workers in groups is a reflection of the pervasiveness of group life in society. Although emphasis is rightly placed on the need for individuals to be treated as such, many clients are unaccustomed to such special attention and feel more comfortable in a group situation. Moreover, it is known that group membership is a powerful source of influence on the individual members involved and therefore may be a potent means of help in the context of social work practice. Thus the justification for working with groups is that this approach is well suited to the needs of some clients, provided, as in all other dimensions, the objectives are clear and the social worker possesses the relevant understanding and skills. It should also be noted that in some situations, particularly in community work, the social worker spends much of his time in working with ready-formed groups, such as committees and associations.

There are naturally many similarities between work with groups and work with families. The family itself is a group, albeit of a somewhat special nature, and many of the points made in the previous section are relevant in the present context. It is of great assistance to the social worker if he is acquainted with theories about small group behaviour, which provide enlightenment and understanding about the various types of interaction he witnesses in practice. One theory of particular importance is that which distinguishes two different levels of behaviour in groups, the instrumental and the expressive. All groups have a task, however loosely defined, and that is usually the principal reason for the existence of the group and provides the basis for the work it does. Behaviour which is directed towards the achievement of the group's task is described as instrumental. On the other hand, people also join groups for reasons other than the desire to reach a goal. They seek emotional satisfactions from belonging to the group and from the relationships they are able to establish within it, behaviour fulfilling these functions being described as expressive. These two aspects of group behaviour may not be counter-productive. In an ideal situation they each contribute to the overall goal, but there is a tendency for them to fall out of balance and sometimes expressive behaviour may threaten the continued existence of the group if it becomes dominant. The social worker needs to be alert to the presence of both instrumental and expressive behaviour in groups, so that he can help members to maintain an effective balance between them.

Group work, like family work, involves the social worker in concern about two types of relationship: that between himself and the group and the relationships between the members. It is therefore important that the size of the group should be such as to facilitate rather than inhibit these relationships and figures of between four and twelve are often suggested as appropriate, the ideal being about seven or eight. In some situations, however, it is possible to manage larger numbers effectively. Much depends on the role which the social worker adopts and this in turn depends on the type of group and the purpose for which it is established. The range of possibilities is enormous and includes those groups which are primarily concerned with engaging in activities (such as play, craft work, outdoor expeditions); those which combine activity with examination of problems of mutual concern (such as socio-drama and other forms of role-playing); those which exist for learning purposes (such as groups of prospective foster-parents or adopters); and those in which the emphasis is on the discussion of common problems, both interpersonal and environmental (such as those for addicts and sex-offenders on the one hand and tenants' associations and community action groups on the other). There are many other kinds of group, notably those arranged by voluntary societies, such as Alcoholics Anonymous and the specialist psychotherapy groups conducted mainly by psychiatrists but occasionally by suitably qualified and experienced social workers. There are also the various kinds of formal and informal groups that arise in day and residential centres and with which social workers are often concerned.

As in work with individuals and families, the roles it is possible for the social worker to adopt in a group situation are infinitely varied according to the strategies of intervention being used. In studies of group work, these roles have been variously described as leader, worker, enabler, conductor, facilitator, encourager and central person, each having different shades of meaning, though often overlapping in practice. The approach of the social worker is dependent primarily on the needs and situation of the group and varies from the directiveness implied by the term 'leader' to the more permissive connotations of other terms. Thus a group of boisterous children may need a relatively high degree of control and therefore of leadership, whereas with a tenants' association the social worker may need to adopt the less directive role of enabler. Furthermore, as the needs of the group change, the relationship with the worker and his role within it alter accordingly. Thus the degree of directiveness he employs must be flexibly related to the processes taking place. Some social workers find it helpful to share group work with a colleague, often one of the opposite sex, which provides further opportunities for flexibility of roles, though it is essential that they establish between themselves very clear agreement about matters such as direction and control if consistency in practice is to be achieved.

Groups have one great advantage over work with individuals in that they provide a multi-dimensional treatment milieu in which members may learn from their relationships with each other as well as with the social worker. For the worker himself, there is usually less chance to dominate the relationship with the client and this enhances the possibility of establishing a genuine partnership in ,the social work process. In addition, the knowledge and strengths of individual members are made available for the benefit of all. Thus each group member has opportunities both to receive help and to give it. Part of the skill of the social worker lies in facilitating this process, beginning by encouraging and enabling people to develop relationships with each other. Other areas of skill are helping members to plan the group's work effectively, supporting them in the process of achieving the group aim, particularly when progress is impeded, helping them to deal with their own conflicts and providing a point of stability on which they can rely.

There are many other aspects of work with groups discussed in the literature, including the question of fixed or changing membership and the problem of whether to arrange a set number of meetings or to continue indefinitely. Like most other issues, these can only be resolved in the context of practice and experience, in which the nature and needs of the group are balanced against the resources available, in terms of time and facilities. There is also a difference between groups established with a limited purpose in terms of the agency's responsibilities, such as short-term activity or discussion groups for offenders; and those which one started go on to develop a continuing life of their own, requiring eventually no more than minimal support from a social worker. Some examples of these are groups for the physically handicapped or for patients discharged from psychiatric hospitals, together with the many different types of community group that become established as self-supporting organisations. Finally, it is helpful to make a distinction between groups established by social workers specifically to achieve certain objectives, whether by discussion, activity or a mixture of both; and those which arise as a consequence of living arrangements (as in a residential centre) or shared activities (as in a day centre). In the latter, there may at times be opportunities for group work in a formally established sense, but social workers must also be skilled in working informally with groups that are not too rigidly defined and which may sometimes arise spontaneously. As in all of their work, they must be ready to seize and use opportunities for intervention as they arise.

The Environment

In Chapter 8, it was indicated that social work practice involves a great deal more than direct work with clients. Many problems have to be tackled and resolved in a societal context that involves the social worker in relationships with individuals, organisations and public bodies that provide the resources necessary to the achievement of his tasks. It is therefore of the utmost importance that social workers should be adept at establishing positive contacts with these individuals and organisations and also be able to maintain a working partnership with them that enables both sides to work effectively. Partnership implies confidence and trust and also the possibility that the disagreements and conflicts that inevitably occur from time to time can be discussed rationally and resolved, rather than leading to an accumulation of mutual antipathy. Lack of understanding of other people's points of view and of the constraints under which they work, together with bias and prejudice, lead all too often to disruptive relationships that rarely result in the client's interests being served. These considerations are of especial significance for community workers for whom the environment is often the centre of their concerns, both as a focus and as the main dimension in which they intervene. Accordingly, they require highly developed skills in forming and using relationships with a wide variety of people, most of whom are not formally designated as clients.

By the very nature of their work and the types of problem with which their clients are confronted, social workers are frequently brought into contact with members of other professions, notably medicine and the law. Professionals are reputed to guard with some jealousy the boundaries of their concerns and social work as a junior aspirant to professional status is sometimes regarded with suspicion if not resentment, because it seems to threaten established methods of dealing with problems. This is only the negative aspect, however, of a situation that contains many promising developments, including the relationships that have been built up over the years in such settings as hospitals, child guidance clinics and the courts, where teamwork is well established. Similar kinds of teamwork may also be found in the relationships with many official bodies and their representatives, notably those whose activities directly affect the welfare of social workers' clients, such as local authority housing and education departments and the offices of the Supplementary Benefits Commission and the Department of Employment. Besides these, there are many other bodies, in varying degrees official or informal, such as voluntary organisations, committees, working parties and planning groups with which social workers become involved and to which they may contribute more effectively if they use their skills in relationships to make the necessary human contacts. These skills are also of special relevance in situations in which the social worker is involved in a public performance, for example when speaking to a court of law about an offender or advocating at a public meeting the need for community support for a new venture. Few social workers appear to be skilled in public speaking, an area that might well benefit from attention in training courses.

Above all, it is vital for social workers to establish constructive working relationships with their colleagues in the same agency and their fellow-professionals in other similar departments. This includes exploring the possibilities of teamwork in situations in which it is still all too common for each social worker to guard jealously his own caseload of clients and to resent suggestions of shared responsibility. It also involves a great deal of attention being given to the relationship between field workers and the staff of residential centres. This is frequently characterised by mutual suspicion and resentment that produce an unwillingness to work co-operatively for the well-being of the client. It is not at all easy to devise ways in which these tense relationships may be resolved, but the possibility of greater movement between the two types of employment arising out of the unification of training arrangements and qualifications is perhaps the best hope, coupled with active attempts, especially by senior staff on both sides, to find local remedies. It is also necessary to consider ways in which teamwork may be more actively promoted within residential centres, where staff are thrown together for far longer periods than in field work and usually in situations that produce greater stress.

Conclusion

In concluding the discussion of relationships in social work that has filled these two chapters, it seems helpful to reiterate the fundamental importance of personality. The social worker is not a mirror, reflecting the client so that he may see himself more clearly, but a person who becomes actively involved in the solution of difficulties brought to him. If he is to establish effective working relationships it is necessary that he should reveal something of himself, not introducing his own problems, which would only confuse the situation, but indicating by manner, behaviour and gesture that he is a real person, a human being with his own interests and ideas and a warm concern for people in trouble. The possession and use of a sense of humour is by no means the least of these qualities and, together with the capacity to share enjoyment at people's successes, is of great assistance in removing some of the fantasies about social workers that develop in the minds of frightened and confused clients.

11

Transactions in Social Work

Some social workers appear to have a natural flair for forming constructive relationships with clients, seemingly without much effort being required. Others, though less favourably endowed by nature, seem to develop similar capacities as a result of learning and experience. For many more, the creation and use of professional relationships is a task that demands the employment of all their personal resources in the face of many obstacles. It therefore seems important to emphasise that although the use of personality is fundamental to effective social work practice, there are certain related skills, the acquisition of which provides support to the central task of forming and sustaining relationships. These skills may be learned and perfected through practice and are associated with what happens when social workers and clients meet face to face and engage in transactions.

The word 'transactions' is used in this context to describe the process of exchange that takes place in meetings between social workers and clients. It is used in preference to the term 'interview', which has the more restricted connotation of a one-sided conversation in which the social worker is the dominant partner. Although it is clearly the responsibility of the social worker to create a situation in which the transactions between himself and the client are directed to positive ends, it has already been emphasised in a number of places in this book that he should attempt to do so on a basis of partnership, involving the client as fully as possible in the process. A further limitation of the term 'interview' is that it is usually applied to meetings involving one or at most a few clients. Since one of the skills of the social worker is his ability to make rapid changes of orientation from individuals to groups, from groups to pairs and so on, it seems inappropriate to describe all such meetings as interviews but all involve transactions. Furthermore, the skills involved in transactions appear to be the same whatever the number of clients concerned and whatever the purpose of the meeting. These skills are basically those related to communication but choices also have to be made about the form in which transactions take place.

Communication Skills

If the purposes of social work are to be fulfilled, it is clearly of the utmost importance that effective communication be established between social workers and their clients. It is the social worker's responsibility to facilitate this by using appropriate skills. Effective communication usually requires an atmosphere of trust in which clients feel confident in speaking about difficulties or making requests and for this reason special attention must be paid to the point at which contact is established for the first time. The social worker has to convey to the client an interest in his problems, a concern to help and a willingness to give time and attention to him. He also needs to demonstrate that he is the kind of person who is receptive to the worries, difficulties and anxieties of the client and is prepared to deal with them objectively, without passing judgement or being disrespectful. These requirements apply as much to dealing with the social problems of communities as to the difficulties of individual clients and families undergoing emotional stress, since it is always important for the social worker to demonstrate quickly the reality of his concern and willingness to help find an answer. They also apply equally to situations in which the client has taken the initiative in seeking help and to those where the social worker intervenes in the course of carrying out statutory requirements. The nature of concern and receptiveness to others is such that it depends entirely on the presence of a real caring basis in the personality of the social worker. For this reason, it is tinged with individual factors that make a general prescription impossible, since each social worker develops his own distinctive ways of receiving clients and putting them at their ease. Nevertheless, courtesy, kind words and gestures and attempts to ensure that clients are seated comfortably in an atmosphere that is warm both physically and psychologically are all aspects of reception that go far to create a sound basis for the development of effective communication. In many agencies the process is further assisted by the skilful behaviour of experienced reception staff, who can do much to allay the anxieties of clients approaching social workers for help for the first time.

From the moment of meeting the client, the social worker is also receiving from him signals that indicate the nature of the problem and the reasons for seeking help. Some of these signals are manifested in visual form and it is therefore important that social workers should be skilled observers of behaviour. This includes watching for signs of physical tension, such as wringing of hands, colouring of the face or restlessness. When more than one client is involved, it also includes noting the looks and gestures that pass between people, which may give clues to the difficulties of a family or group. In a broader context, it is necessary for social workers to be skilled observers of the social scene, familiar with the physical and economic conditions of the various environments from which their clients come, for these are often vital components of the client's problems that must be recognised and understood. Other signals from the client take the form of the words in which he attempts to communicate the nature of his problems. Many people find it extremely difficult to talk clearly about what is troubling them, presenting a confused and disorganised account of which the social worker can make little sense. It is sometimes possible to elucidate the problem by careful prompting, returning to points that seem to be inadequately explained, but it is wise to beware of using this technique in the very early stages of contact since it may close the door to further communication. It is better for the social worker to tolerate confusion for a time, as once good communication has been established, aspects that lack clarity can be raised again for further clarification.

In receiving the word signals transmitted by the client, the primary skill of the social worker lies in the ability to listen effectively. Listening is in fact a dual skill involving the ability to hear and retain the words spoken and also to receive whatever meaning may lie beneath them, the 'music behind the words' as it is sometimes called. Even in a one-to-one relationship, the task of listening is never a simple one, but when several or many people are involved, as in work with groups and in the community, it becomes still more complex because the social worker needs to be aware of the many possible cross-currents of communication taking place among those present and between them and himself. The ideal listener is able to free his mind of all other concerns and responsibilities apart from those immediately facing him, so that he is able to engage actively and responsively in the process.

The social worker is thus more than a passive receiver of communications from the client. He must be a listener who is able to respond actively and appropriately to the messages he receives. To do this, he requires the ability to assess the relative significance of the various communications received, together with skill in relating them together and making tentative interpretations of their meaning in his own mind. In doing this, he makes use of any other relevant information that he has received from the client's family, the environment and other sources that is likely to enhance his understanding of the situation. Here it is necessary to warn of the danger of imposing one's own interpretation on a situation without paying heed to all the relevant facts. This is a common problem for social workers and can occur for a variety of reasons. Sometimes a new situation reminds the social worker of a similar one previously encountered. It is then all too easy to attribute to the new situation characteristics of the previous one and make a false interpretation of the facts. Other social workers are prone to adopt theoretical standpoints that limit the range of possible interpretations of the client's situation. These standpoints may be narrowly psychodynamic at one extreme or rigidly environmental at the other, with many variations in between, but any doctrinaire interpretation is likely to be unjust to clients whose lives are individual and whose difficulties should therefore be assessed on as broad a basis as possible.

In reacting to communications from clients, the social worker has a wide choice of possible responses. In all cases, however, responses should reflect the two levels on which communication takes place, intellectual and emotional. A careful balance should be maintained between those responses that meet the clients' need for emotional satisfaction, the feeling that they are important and respected, and those which through using the intellect, however limited, lead to a greater understanding of the situation and the search for solutions. All responses are likely to contain elements of both emotion and intellect, so that it is usually the balance between the two with which the social worker is concerned. In some cases the social worker is required to respond very little. This happens when a client is full of suppressed emotion and desires to release it to a sympathetic listener, who need do no more than 'make encouraging noises', as it is sometimes described. There are times when non-verbal communication is a more appropriate means of response than the use of words. An arm around the shoulder of a tearful child or the provision of paper and crayon for drawing a picture may be sufficient demonstrations of care and concern that allow communication channels to develop. In residential and day care there are many opportunities for non-verbal communication as a supplement or alternative to the use of language. One report takes the view that the development of non-verbal methods of helping in residential care could usefully be extended to other forms of social work. 'The skills of home making, of creating rapport through physical contact such as bathing or feeding, of providing constructive ego-building experiences through planned activities, are skills which would be invaluable to social workers who work with clients from a community base.'[1]

In beginning to respond verbally, the social worker may make use of questions designed to elicit further information. It is usually helpful if such questions can be phrased in ways that avoid encouraging answers of one or a few words and instead prompt the client to develop what he has said further. Thus, 'Could you tell me more about what happened?' is an open-ended question that is potentially more revealing than, 'When did it happen?' Sometimes it is useful to make statements that imply a question rather than to ask one directly. 'Some people feel very angry when that kind of thing happens' is a statement that suggests that feelings of anger are permissible and encourages the client to acknowledge them if he wishes, but does not force an open admission or denial.

Further responses take the form of providing information about services and facilities or preparing clients for experiences that they are about to undergo, such as a court appearance or admission to hospital. It is appropriate here to emphasise the importance of clarity about the reasons for the social worker's intervention and the possibilities for help. Confusion between social worker and client sometimes arises because the latter has failed to perceive clearly the reasons for their contact with each other. In situations in which the social worker has taken the initiative in intervention it can be especially important for him to explain the reasons for his presence as soon as he meets the client. In other situations, such as community work, it may be appropriate to allow the reason for intervention to emerge slowly over the course of time, perhaps because the social worker's brief is open-ended and subject to negotiation with the people to be involved. In general, however, it is a good principle to explain to clients the reasons for one's presence, in order to create a sound working basis. A further aspect of this is the importance of conveying to clients the limitations of the social worker and his agency in providing help. Some clients appear to expect that like a conjuror, the social worker will produce magical solutions from a hat, whereas in reality most agencies have strict limitations on powers and resources and it becomes necessary to help clients to grasp this and to encourage them to seek alternative means of help from other agencies and also from their own personal, family and neighbourhood networks.

The social worker's assessment of the situation underlies all the forms of response which he uses, but from time to time it may be appropriate to offer a specific interpretation to the client. In some cases, this is a continuing aspect of the transactions between client and social worker, for example when they are engaged in the promotion of the client's self-understanding, as described in

Chapter 6. In many, if not all cases, however, there are times when it is appropriate for a social worker to describe to an individual or group how he perceives their problem or behaviour as a further stimulus to the search for a solution. In part, this is a feature of the confrontation strategy described in Chapter 7, but it is also relevant to other methods of intervention as a means of feeding back to the client aspects of attitudes or behaviour that might enhance his understanding of his problems. Interpretation of this kind is a delicate task. It needs to be sensitively matched to the client's capacity to accept it or else it will be ignored or seen as criticism and attack. Although the latter is not necessarily counter-productive in the long run, it is easy to touch accidentally on feelings of guilt or hostility that the client is suppressing because for the moment that is the only way he can manage them. Although this may sometimes have positive results, there is a strong risk that the effect will be the production of a more severely defensive reaction that hinders communication and undermines the relationship between social worker and client. Defence mechanisms are a necessary possession for satisfactory social life and social workers should beware of attacking them directly. If they appear to be a handicap to the client, it is usually more appropriate to work in less direct ways, using enabling strategies to build up self-respect and increase personal satisfactions to the point where it is no longer necessary for the defences to be so rigidly maintained.

All transactions in social work are limited by exigencies of time. Social workers have a responsibility to ensure that meetings with clients are brought to a satisfactory conclusion. It can be useful if, towards the end of a meeting, the social worker summarises what appears to have happened during the discussion and follows this by making plans with the client for future meetings, if these appear to be needed. When further meetings are contemplated, it is sometimes helpful if social worker and client agree that in the meantime each will give some thought to the problems being tackled in preparation for the next discussion. They may also need to devote time to planning the structure and content of future meetings, particularly in the group and community context. Finally, they may need to make decisions about action to be taken in the interim by social worker or client, such as writing letters or contacting other agencies and organisations. It may be helpful for some of this to be recorded in writing as suggested in Chapter 3.

The same courtesy and kindliness that characterise the social worker's approach at the start of a meeting are normally relevant to its conclusion. It is obviously helpful if the client leaves feeling that the meeting has been a worthwhile experience, though that may not necessarily happen for a number of reasons, some of which, such as misconceptions of the agency's function, have already been mentioned. Other reasons may be the social worker's lack of skill in dealing with a particular client or his inability to provide an immediate solution to a problem of long-standing. Finally, dissatisfaction may arise because of the presence of transactional difficulties.

Some Transactional Difficulties

Most social workers are literate and fluent in speech. They are accustomed to starting conversations with a wide variety of people and experience little difficulty in establishing rapport. Not all of their clients, however, are able to respond so readily. Some are nervous or frightened, but may be helped to talk freely in a relaxed and encouraging atmosphere. Others are handicapped by deficiencies in intellect and education that make it difficult for them to find the right words to express their problems, or by physical limitations such as deafness or blindness that require the use of specialist communication skills for effective understanding to be achieved. Furthermore, clients may be completely baffled by the language used by the social worker that reflects a different and perhaps more privileged background. Such people require a great deal of patience on the part of the social worker in allowing and enabling them to grope for the right words slowly and disjointedly without being hurried. The social worker must also be able to choose his own words carefully, using terms that the client will have a chance of understanding. Clients who are bemused by fluency in language may easily give the impression of understanding, sometimes out of a desire to please, when in fact they are completely lost, so care as well as patience is needed to ensure that effective communication is taking place. This is particularly likely to occur when language problems are so great that there is a complete barrier to communication. In working with immigrants, the social worker may be handicapped by the lack of a common tongue in which they can converse and be obliged to communicate through other members of the family or an interpreter, in the process of which misunderstandings can easily arise. There is no easy solution to this problem, though in areas with large numbers of immigrant clients it would seem sensible for social work agencies to employ staff who can speak the appropriate languages.

Social workers are usually rational in their approach to life's problems and may have feelings of impatience with those whose thought processes and behaviour are less logical. Many clients follow emotion rather than reason as a guide to behaviour, a course which often exacerbates rather than alleviates their difficulties. Thus although it may seem appropriate to encourage clients to think before they act, not all are able to develop this capacity. It may therefore be necessary for social workers to accept the chaos and irrationality that is characteristic of some people's lives and concentrate on creating supports in the family and environment that will minimise the harmful effects of such behaviour. Thus a family caring for a mentally retarded child might be encouraged to hand over pocket money in small daily amounts instead of in a weekly sum that would be spent immediately. In working with a community group, the creation of a committee structure and procedural rules may help to reduce the tendency of individuals to act impulsively in ways that are contrary to the group's objectives.

Sometimes clients use social workers as targets at which to fire suppressed negative feelings. This may take the form of generalised hostility against all those in authority or it may be more personal in nature, directed towards what is perceived as some failure on the part of the social worker. As was indicated in Chapter 9, it is part of the social worker's role to accept and encourage the expression of negative feelings, when it appears to be in the interests of the client that these should be released, but this is not easy to do in practice. Skilful handling of hostility requires the ability to accept the reality of the feelings involved without condemnation or rejection, and the willingness to recognise the justification for them when it exists. Once exposed for discussion, hostile feelings often seem less frightening to both client and worker and they also provide a basis for greater honesty in the professional relationship, from which may develop changed perceptions and different approaches to the resolution of problems.

The hostile client has the merit of providing a ready opening to communication. In contrast, the silent or withdrawn client presents a much greater problem for the social worker, particularly if his predominant mood is one of apathy. It needs to be said here that silences may occur in the course of any human transactions, but not always for the same reason. Some silences are hostile, some indicate embarrassment and some represent a pause in which the people concerned are engaging in constructive thought prior to further discussion. Social workers require skill in understanding the nature of any particular silence and responding appropriately. In the case of thoughtful silences it is particularly important to be able to refrain from interruption that breaks an important chain of thought, so that the client is free to resume conversation when he is ready.

Clients who are withdrawn and speak very little may be naturally so or they may be suffering from some kind of mental disorder such as depression or psychosis. Some may be encouraged to speak if the social worker talks to them patiently in a way that demonstrates a wish to communicate with and understand them. Others find it possible to start talking if the social worker ceases to concentrate intensively on them and seeks to establish communication through some other medium, an approach that is particularly valuable in work with children, who often find it very difficult to relate directly to adults. Interest in a toy or in the social worker's car may provide a safe and comfortable focus for the start of communication that may lead to more personal matters later. Alternatively, a shared activity, such as a game or an excursion, may provide the foundation for communication and this approach may be used with people of all ages. In dealing with clients who are withdrawn or apathetic, it is also important to consider the relevance of working in different dimensions of intervention. Many adolescent offenders are uncomfortable in a one-to-one relationship with an adult, but can accept membership of a group in which their need for support from their peers is met. Similarly, many other clients, such as those who are physically handicapped or elderly, may be more responsive to a group approach.

There are some clients with whom it appears to be impossible to establish effective communication at all, however persistent and understanding the social worker's approach. Some are so seriously disturbed that they have withdrawn into a world of their own, exhibiting bizarre symptoms of which little sense can be made. In dealing with such clients, it is very easy to take more notice of peculiarities than of efforts to behave normally, thus reinforcing the disordered behaviour. Although the prospects of establishing effective communication may be limited, it is worth trying an approach based on learning theory in which positive, coping behaviour is praised and encouraged and bizarre symptoms ignored as far as is possible. Relatives may be helped to adopt a similar pattern of behaviour as a further means of restoring the client's social functioning. Finally, there are other clients whose beliefs, values, culture and general style of life may lead them to see the work of the social worker as alien to their interests. Some may be immigrants who wish to maintain their own culture intact in a strange land. Others may have political, religious or ideological reasons which prevent them from co-operating with the social worker. The professional view of such clients is that they have the right to be respected for their beliefs and that they are not obliged to accept help, though the offer should be made in case they wish to change their views. In general, they would then be left to manage unaided, but in circumstances where they are causing trouble to others or breaking the law, the social worker may well be required to intervene officially, however unpromising the prospects for effective work.

Sensitive awareness of the feelings and needs of others is a key factor in helping the social worker to decide on appropriate dimensions and strategies of intervention. It is also of great value in the process of assessment. This kind of awareness is sometimes described as intuition, since although it is based in part on information received from the client and the environment, it contains an element that can only be described as imaginative hunch. This aspect springs from the social worker's own reactions to clients which, if carefully analysed, make an important contribution to the understanding of behaviour. The direct expression of these reactions must usually be restrained for professional reasons, but awareness of them is a great aid in assessment. Thus, when a social worker feels frustrated or angry with a client, this may be an indication of the effect that the latter has on many other people in his life and thus be a substantial element in creating his difficulties. It is sometimes possible to play back this type of reaction in the form of an interpretation, as was discussed above. At other times, there may be less clearly demonstrable evidence, but simply a feeling that the client has a particular attitude or problem. The social worker must then find ways of introducing this possibility into the discussion, perhaps in the form of a general statement, perhaps in a way that points it more directly at the client. There is always a risk that a hunch will prove wrong, but it can provide a useful technique, particularly when an impasse seems to have been reached. The social worker should thus use his own feelings about clients and the way they behave as a means of increasing his understanding and, with caution and care, as a way of promoting the client's welfare.

Transactional Choices

In setting the scene for transactions between himself and clients, the social worker has a number of choices to make, in some of which he may also be able to involve the client as a participant. As is suggested elsewhere in this book, it is first of all necessary to choose which dimension provides the most relevant approach for intervention, whether it be individual, pair, family, group or the environment. Although some take the view that it is important to avoid mixing dimensions, ensuring, for example, that in a group situation all problems are contained and dealt with in the group, experience suggests the need for flexibility. This implies the use of a multi-dimensional approach, with flexibility of choice at any one time and exclusive concentration on a specific dimension only if the need is clearly indicated. The choice of dimension is invariably dependent on the needs of the client, the views of the social worker and the resources available. Any one of these may rule out a particular approach in a specific case and the availability of resources is especially influential in the group dimension, because of the need for accommodation and possibly for materials and equipment, none of which may be readily available.

The same considerations affect choice of venue. Transactions may take place at the social worker's office, in the client's home, in a residential or day centre, or anywhere else that seems suitable, including community centres, cafés and public houses. Each type of venue has its own special characteristics and it is often desirable to use a combination of venues for different purposes. The social worker's office may seem formidable and frightening to some clients, but for others it is a haven of peace and helpfulness in a chaotic world. The office has the advantage of being separate from the environmental pressures that affect the client's home, but it is not always accessible owing to distance and lack of suitable transport. For this reason, much social work in Britain takes place in the client's home, where there may be distractions and lack of concentration on the reasons for the social worker's visit. This is sometimes counterbalanced by the presence of other family members and the opportunity to work in more than one dimension, leading to enhanced understanding of the situation. Most social workers find that they need to be skilled in conducting the transactional process in the face of competition for the client's attention from other family members, the television set and general domestic activity.

Another area of choice is concerned with the form that transactions take. Are they arranged by appointment or do they occur on a casual basis in response to more immediate need? Most social workers prefer to leave room for both contingencies, but if the profession is to establish itself convincingly in the public eye, it seems important that due regard should be given to making appointments which recognise the need for individual attention at a special time. Working to a system of appointments also allows the social worker time to prepare for each meeting with the client and may help to ensure the absence of distractions during the course of their encounters. The frequency and length of meetings is also an important consideration. When ongoing work is needed, weekly meetings can be valuable as a longer gap allows the momentum to run down to a point at which time is wasted restoring it at the start of each meeting. This is particularly important in working with groups, but it also applies to any other dimensions when the work is of an intensive nature. In situations in which the main strategy is one of oversight, contact may justifiably become infrequent. In contrast, when problems are pressing to the point of crisis, daily contact may be necessary, as in work with families facing eviction or with offenders newly discharged from penal institutions. The length of individual meetings must be related to their purpose in the context of the total plan of intervention. For some meetings a few minutes suffice, whereas others require concentration for an hour or more on the needs of an individual or a group. In day and residential centres transactions may take the form of continuous or intermittent contact between workers and clients without any set meeting periods. In these circumstances, it is important that staff should give thought to the planning of each day's programme in such a way that it provides opportunities for transactions between individuals and in groups, both formally and informally, on a flexible basis that meets the varied needs of the clients concerned.

All of the considerations relating to the management of transactions require skill, but it is not possible to state specifically what should and should not be done. The same points apply to transactions in the environment, in which the social worker is involved with other individuals and agencies. For these aspects of the work he requires not only the skills already discussed, such as the ability to observe and listen, the capacity to interpret and respond appropriately, but also other qualities such as a good speaking voice and expertise in advocacy. In all situations, the choices made must depend upon the social worker's individual assessment of need and of the most appropriate strategies for intervention, but it is essential that decisions should be made on a rational and planned basis, rather than being left to chance.

12

Organisational Skills

Social workers lay great emphasis on their primary concern with the problems and needs of the client and this is reflected in the discussion of skills in the last three chapters. Skills in relationships and transactions have been examined from a client-centred standpoint, as if the social worker is for the most part free to choose the dimensions in which he operates and to decide his own balance between different strategies of intervention. It is true that for much of the time, social workers have considerable freedom of choice about the way in which they work and can thus provide an individual service carefully matched to the needs of each client, but they are also subject to certain constraints that arise from the nature of their employment. These constraints are particularly significant in relation to the taking of decisions that control the services given to clients, but they also have wider implications for social work practice. It is the argument of this chapter that to be effective practitioners, social workers require skills that enable them to carry out their professional activities in an organisational context. These skills are dependent on understanding the characteristics of organisations in general and on the function of the social worker's specific employing agency, including his role within it and his administrative responsibilities.

Characteristics of Organisations

An organisation exists to fulfil a function in society and as such may serve communal or sectional interests. In the case of social work organisations, the function is usually a communal one in that they are funded from public sources and theoretically available to anyone requiring the services they provide. All organisations have goals, which are stated with varying degrees of clarity. Although one goal may be predominant at a given time, it is common for there to be a multiplicity of interrelated goals, all of which the organisation attempts to serve in varying degrees. Thus an industrial concern producing material goods aims to realise a profit for shareholders, but is also concerned with meeting consumer needs, providing employment and playing a part in the general economic structure of the country in which it exists. Social work organisations are no different from this in that they also have a multiplicity of goals, some of which are related to helping specific individuals and groups, while others are concerned with the needs of society as a whole. They also contribute indirectly to social welfare by providing employment and although that is not perhaps a primary goal, it is an undeniable characteristic of any social work organisation.

Goals may be divided into aims and objectives. The former are concerned with the direction in which the organisation wishes to move and as such tend to be non-specific and difficult to translate into practical terms. Thus in Scotland, the departments of social work have a statutory responsibility to promote social welfare, an aim which in theory could include every activity of every individual and group that is instigated with some positive philanthropic intention, together with much of the work of industry, commerce, business and government. Although the personal social services in England, Wales and Northern Ireland do not have such a wide-ranging brief, certain acts of parliament require them to undertake comprehensive responsibilities in relation to the general welfare of specific client groups, such as children and the elderly. It is obviously impossible to organise the work of an agency such as a social services department in ways that can be clearly seen to fulfil such global aims. Consequently, it is necessary to specify a range of objectives that can be expected to contribute to the achievement of the overall aims. This is perhaps more easily achieved in an industrial context, where input in terms of labour and processes can be clearly linked to output in terms of finished products on which a monetary value can be placed.

In the field of social welfare, objectives tend to be less specific, but that does not mean that they are absent. Some can be linked with the intentions of legislation, which often indicates the desirability of certain kinds of action. As an example of this, the Children and Young Person's Act, 1963, enabled local authorities to take action to avoid the need for children to be received into care, thereby endorsing an objective relating to preventive work that had emerged in practice in the preceding years. Changes of national policy may also be expressed in regulations or in papers that recommend a specific pattern of developments. In 1971, a government paper concerned with services for the mentally retarded[1] established more firmly the objective of restoring to community care a substantial number of those living in long-stay hospitals.

Although it is often necessary to use terms such as 'substantial' or 'more' in setting objectives for the social services, in some situations it is possible to be more specific. This is certainly the case when accommodation for day or residential care is concerned, since it must be planned and constructed on the basis of estimates of need, including projections into the future. In their ten-year plans, local authority social services departments specify the expected nature of developments in domiciliary, fieldwork, day care and residential services which may be taken as an embodiment of some aspects of their goals. Similarly, probation and after-care departments must make plans for the future scope of their services that include both staffing and the provision of accommodation of an increasingly varied nature, including after-care and bail hostels and day training centres. Some would argue that such long-term planning is useless, since changing needs cannot be forecast with any degree of accuracy, whereas plans once agreed become commitments that are unalterable. It is therefore important to emphasise that such planning must be tentative and subject to modification in the light of experience and of social changes. Even so, no organisation can exist without a certain amount of forward planning and this requires careful study and analysis if it is to embody more than a continuance of existing provision.

A further important point about objectives in social welfare agencies is that they spring not only from legislation and public pronouncements but are also firmly based on values about what are and are not appropriate methods of meeting need. At times this creates irrational effects, demonstrated for example in the competition between local authority children's departments in the years after 1948 to produce the highest ratio of children boarded out in foster homes. This reflected an understandable but somewhat irrational reaction to the Curtis Report[2] that led social workers to oppose the use of residential institutions for the care of children except as a last resort. Subsequently, the dislike of residential care has spread to social workers' dealings with other client groups, such as the elderly, the physically handicapped and offenders, but although institutions clearly have their limitations, the desire to dispense with them should be founded on the absence of client need rather than on professional prejudice. Values also have more subtle effects on organisational objectives than the examples given above, since they represent the social worker's view of society and have implications for change involving the redistribution of resources, as was suggested in Chapter 1 of this book.

Social work organisations vary in the extent to which their goals are intrinsic or are part of a wider and perhaps different range of objectives. Thus social services and probation and after-care departments may be seen as existing primarily to fulfil social work objectives, on which they are free to concentrate most of their resources. It is true that the former, in particular, encompasses other functions such as the provision of home help and meals-on-wheels services, but these are closely connected with the main task and fit appropriately into a general programme of intervention. In contrast, there are social work departments that exist in an ancillary capacity in larger organisations that have objectives that extend beyond welfare. In the hospital situation, the social work department, a section of the local authority social services department, fulfils an ancillary welfare function in relation to the primary task, which is the medical one of treatment and cure. Similarly, probation officers seconded to work in prisons operate in an ancillary capacity in a situation in which welfare work contributes to but is not the main function of the organisation, that being containment and rehabilitation through custody, control, work and other activities. Social work in an ancillary capacity is no less valid than it is elsewhere, but there are implications for skill in terms of the ability to work in a multi-disciplinary team. There are also implications for objectives which may have to be modified in the light of considerations outside the sphere of social work. As an example, the objective of establishing a programme of group work for prisoners in a certain penal institution may be achievable in only limited terms because of lack of resources in the prison and if there are disturbances or escapes, the entire scheme may have to be sacrificed to considerations of security. In these ancillary situations, social work is perhaps more exposed and therefore more demands are made on its practitioners to specify the objectives of their department and win the co-operation of other officials in the organisation in their fulfilment.

Whatever its size and whether it exists as an entity in its own right or is part of a larger organisation with different objectives, a social work agency resembles all other organisations in requiring a structure to enable it to fulfil its functions. In common with most other organisations in Britain, social work agencies have shown a tendency to develop hierarchical structures that provide for the allocation of differing degrees of responsibility according to rank and also allow for differential allocation of work on a specialist basis. Such structures are usually designed to ensure that there is adequate control of resources and that the staff of the organisation can be held accountable for the work they do, thus satisfying the committee which is given the overall responsibility for providing the service and represents the public's interest in the oversight of expenditure. The advantages of this system for the social worker lie mainly in the fact that it provides a means of access to resources within the department. Since these resources are usually scarce, it is necessary to provide a bureaucratic system of rationing them. Thus, the provision of a home help service or of residential accommodation is subjected to managerial control in order to ensure some degree of justice in their allocation. Other advantages are contained in provisions for supervision and support from more experienced staff to those who are still learning the practice of social work, together with the possibility of allocating work on a basis that is rational and appropriate to the interests and abilities of the individual worker. This latter aspect is discussed in a subsequent section on the place of specialisation.

It must be said that the apparent advantages of organisational membership are not always perceived as such by social workers, who often find it restricting and frustrating, a handicap rather than a help in carrying out their tasks. It is often suggested that social work requires a new type of organisational structure that is not hierarchical, but to date none has been invented and successfully implemented, even though in some voluntary agencies, such as Family Service Units, bureaucratic constraints are usually much less apparent than in statutory services. Whether or not a new type of structure can be devised, it is important to find ways of increasing the individual social worker's range of autonomy, in order to maximise work satisfaction and provide the greatest possible flexibility in offering services to the client. It is noteworthy that the staff who provide services directly to clients in both field and residential work occupy the lowest positions in the organisational hierarchy and in many respects have the least power. As front-line workers, they are in some senses the most important members of the agency and it seems regrettable that promotion usually involves giving up work with clients in order to undertake administrative and managerial tasks which, important though they are, involve substantial changes of function and the learning of new skills.

Agency Function and Organisational Roles

It should not be thought that the social worker is altogether powerless, since for much of his work he depends on his own skill and knowledge rather than on agency resources and the smooth functioning of the bureaucratic system. In face-to-face work with clients, he is remarkably free to operate as he wishes in terms of the exploration and assessment of need and many of the strategies of intervention discussed in this book require only his own resources for effective application. Moreover, skills and methods in social work are relevant to work in any type of agency, though they may be used differentially, according to the specific tasks involved. Agency function is thus more important in determining the nature of the work done than in influencing the skills and methods employed.

Until recently, the most common type of social work agency or department was one with a fairly well-defined specialist function. The history of social work is characterised by the continuing emergence of specialist organisations to meet specific needs, usually at first on a voluntary basis, but with increasing statutory involvement as the case became established for more substantial and comprehensive provision. The probation and after-care service provides a good example of this process. Beginning with the work of temperance organisations in the later part of the nineteenth century, interest gradually spread to a wider concern with the needs of offenders in general as well as of those charged with drunkenness, and culminated in the statutory implementation of the probation service in 1907. Since that time, the service has expanded its functions enormously, added 'after-care' to its title, moved into prison welfare work and adopted a stance in which it displays general concern for the care of the offender in the community. Nevertheless, in spite of the fact that it has acquired other duties related to the courts, such as matrimonial conciliation and divorce court welfare, it has retained a clear specialist identity in being primarily concerned with social work with offenders and their families. This clarity of function is of great assistance to workers in the service in deciding on their aims and objectives in specific cases and in determining the type of resources which are required.

Prior to the reorganisation of local authority social services and the further changes resulting from local government reorganisation in the nineteen seventies, many other services were established on a specialist basis with a reasonably clear identity. Among these were the local authority children's, mental health and social welfare departments and the social work departments in general and psychiatric hospitals. The creation of new departments with comprehensive responsibilities for personal social services was accompanied by the concept of a generic social worker, capable of undertaking the entire range of tasks in relation to every need group, but it is debatable whether it is within the capacity of any individual to encompass such a wide variety of functions. The Seebohm Committee's Report envisaged a general social worker at basic level but also emphasised the need for consultants to undertake specialist work of greater complexity. To date, the latter have emerged mainly in an advisory capacity, with the result that at basic level, where the newest recruits are found, there is a serious lack of specialist expertise. One of the reasons for this may be confusion about the meaning of the term 'generic'. It was originally used, as indicated in Chapter 2, to emphasise common elements in the training of social workers for different specialisms, but it has come to be interpreted as a comprehensive ability to tackle every kind of work. That is plainly unrealistic, since it is the skills and methods of social work that are generic, not the knowledge of the social worker, which consists of specialised elements related to particular kinds of problems and needs, according to interest and experience. Social workers inevitably develop special interests in working with particular client groups or in specialist settings, such as hospitals or community work, for which they require much more detailed knowledge related to the nature of the work involved. Provided that within a general agency sufficient coverage is given to the total range of work, it seems sensible and appropriate to allow specialisms to develop where possible.

The argument of this section is therefore that opportunities to specialise are desirable both to satisfy the interests of social workers and also to ensure the provision to the client of a service of adequate standard. In some circumstances, specialism is obligatory because the nature and structure of the work demand it. This applies to probation officers seconded to work as prison welfare officers and also to hospital social work, even though that is now a local authority responsibility. In other circumstances, it is necessary to provide at the first point of contact with the client a general service capable of producing an all-round assessment of need. This is clearly essential for local authority departments, but it does not necessarily mean that all staff must operate on a general basis. Many departments have found it useful to establish intake systems, in which a team of workers, ideally very experienced since assessment is a highly skilled task, deal with all new referrals from point of contact until a limited period has elapsed. This period may be anything from six weeks to three months, after which only cases needing extensive help for a longer period are passed on to other staff, who may work on a general or specialist basis according to preference and the needs of the department. There are obviously problems about the extent to which it is reasonable to expect social workers to concentrate permanently on intake work which is highly demanding and offers few long-term satisfactions, but this approach seems more rational than a system in which everyone is a multi-purpose worker. Provided that there are opportunities to change function from time to time, it seems desirable to arrange for specialism on a flexible basis and there are clearly other duties in social services departments that lend themselves to concentration of resources in this way. These may or may not be directly related to work of the specialised departments that existed prior to the reorganisation of local authority social services. Thus some specialisms could be based on the needs of groups such as the physically handicapped and the mentally disordered, whereas others might emerge from new functions, such as intermediate treatment programmes for young offenders.

The foregoing discussion has illustrated the close connection between agency function and the role of the social worker within the organisation. Social workers function best when they are clear about their role within the context of the organisation's goals and responsibilities. The agency should aim to facilitate this process and also to protect the social worker from unreasonable demands on his time and other resources, so that he can do his work effectively. Such protection, together with the provision of support and consultation, falls to middle managers in the organisation, themselves usually social workers by profession. Some of the important aspects of an effective support system are discussed in the next section of this chapter.

Organisational Skills

Social work is a highly stressful occupation which constantly drains its practitioners of their personal resources. To enable them to continue coping with the demands of the work and to help them to remain effective as practitioners, social workers need support from two sources: their immediate superiors and their colleagues. This is not a simple matter, since the quality of support is dependent on the ability of those involved to facilitate it, including the person needing the support. Thus, although a senior social worker or senior probation officer has a primary responsibility to create effective working relationships between himself and his staff and within the team as a whole, they themselves must also contribute to the process by operating on a collaborative basis. The foundation for such teamwork is the same as for work with clients, the quality of care and concern that exists among those involved. Social workers who care about their clients must also care about and be cared for by their colleagues, these being the principal contributing factors to effective teamwork. This is not a plea for everlasting harmony of relationships, but for a positive caring environment in which differences may be as freely expressed as agreement. Any social worker who has experienced such a working environment will agree that it involves much perseverance and skill, but that the effort is worthwhile in terms of its rewards, which enable them to work more effectively with clients because of their greater personal insight and confidence.

These elements, insight and confidence, are an important part of the process of consultation and supervision that takes place between social workers and their immediate seniors. It is usual to discuss supervision from the viewpoint of the supervisor, but since this book is primarily concerned with social work at the basic level, the emphasis here is on the recipient. Thus, although the senior is responsible for creating the conditions in which supervision takes place, the social worker plays a major part in making it effective. He must be aware of the opportunities that a supervisory relationship provides and learn how to make use of them in ways that enhance the quality of his work. It is usual to distinguish between consultation and supervision on the basis that in the former the worker takes the initiative and is not bound by any advice given, whereas in the latter the supervisor promotes the process on the basis of his organisational responsibilities and can demand that certain courses of action be followed or rejected. In addition, the supervisor has managerial functions in ensuring that work is properly done, which are no concern of the consultant. These are relevant and important differences, but they do not apply to the central features of both supervision and consultation, which are teaching and enabling. The social worker thus expects to learn from supervision and that includes increasing his knowledge about the problems of clients and the possible means of tackling them, as well as about his own capabilities. He also expects to be helped by the process to undertake work or tackle problems that have hitherto presented difficulties to him and in consequence learns more about himself and his developing professional ability.

A further range of skills in working in an organisation is demanded by the need for social workers to operate in collaboration with others. In part this is related to teamwork, already considered for its supportive aspects, but also important for the ways in which it enables staff to share responsibilities, cover duties for each other and to some extent to substitute for each other in work with clients. Social workers are apt to become possessive about their clients, a feeling that is by no means always reciprocated. Teamwork makes it possible for colleagues to deal with emergencies in the absence of the usual worker and also for any specialists in the team to provide a distinctive contribution from their own standpoint. This aspect is of increasing importance now that it is common for social work teams to contain members with different types of skill from social workers themselves. Thus welfare assistants, ancillary workers and trainees all have contributions to make to the total task and it is important for their specialist attributes to be used wisely and economically.

Social workers may themselves have managerial responsibilities in relation to such workers, among whom may also be included clerical and administrative staff attached to the team. The skilled use of relationships, in an appropriate fashion, is as important in relation to those people as it is to clients. In addition, the resources of a team are sometimes increased by the appointment of voluntary workers, who also require skilled management and deployment if their abilities are to be put to best use.

A further dimension of collaborative work is concerned with the relationship between different sections of organisations. Large agencies are forced to create specialist sections that involve staff at all levels in complex relationships as they seek to obtain resources. Each section tends to develop its own priorities and perceptions and that often leads to conflict with others, which are seen as obstructive and unco-operative, difficulties similar to those that sometimes arise in inter-organisational relationships. Social workers need skill in handling conflict within their agency and also in working on a collaborative basis with other departmental sections. This requires a knowledge of systems, procedures and practices and an understanding of organisational behaviour.

Since organisations are dynamic entities, social workers are also interested in the processes by which change may be achieved. They are commonly critical about matters such as the structure of the departments in which they work and about the constraints imposed by policies and procedures, and this leads them to seek for ways of inducing organisational change. Sometimes, social workers are invited to participate in committees or working parties that have been established to examine aspects of departmental policy with a view to proposing alterations. In some departments, there are standing arrangements for consultation between senior staff and basic level social workers, so that the views of the latter may be taken into account in policy development. It must be admitted, however, that many social workers feel that such opportunities create an illusion of involvement in policy making that belies the reality of the situation. As a result, they may prefer to press for change from outside through their professional associations, but although this provides a valuable alternative, it seems equally important for social workers to use their skills in relationships and in advocacy within their own departments. They should be prepared to collect and sift relevant information that they gather from clients and the environment, using it to establish a case for the changes they consider are required. They might also press for more tangible representation for themselves and clients in the policy making process, encouraging senior staff and the members of the employing committee to enter into more democratic relationships with the recipients of services. There is much work to be done in this area, but the growing interest in community work, together with legislation that gives the client the possibility of a more active role in the provision as well as receipt of services, as in the community service scheme for offenders, suggest that it may be possible to break some of the rigidly defined boundaries and create more truly participative social welfare.

Finally, it is the responsibility of social workers to learn to manage their own resources efficiently. This point is developed further in the discussion of administration which follows, but it also has professional implications. The social worker's main resources are time and skill and it is important that the latter should be maintained and enhanced through discussion with colleagues and consultation with senior staff, together with reading, attending courses and taking part in training and re-training schemes. In accepting the offer of employment by an organisation, the social worker unavoidably surrenders the right to practise as a truly independent professional, but he gains in exchange the opportunity to work in a supportive environment with access to resources and to develop his skills through experience and supervision. If he is to provide the best possible service to the client, he must also develop the organisational skills that enable him to work as one of a team and obtain the resources that are available.

Administration

It is usual for social workers to be accorded a great deal of freedom to plan their work programme on an individual basis. In any particular week, it is likely that there will be certain fixed points, such as a court hearing or a case conference and it is also necessary that social workers should pay due regard to the constraints of employment by a specific agency, discussed in the first part of this chapter. These exceptions apart, the social worker is free to respond to the needs of clients on a flexible basis, provided that his work-load is not so excessive that he is out of control of the situation. It has to be admitted that this is often true, with the result that the social worker's programme is dictated by his clients, particularly by those with the most pressing needs or by those who make the loudest demands, who may receive attention at the expense of others requiring help less urgently or less vocal in making their problems known. Since social work in Britain is a public service, it may be argued that it is right that clients should take the lead in deciding how it should operate, but this approach runs the risk of injustice. When resources are scarce, those with the power to distribute them must take steps to ensure that this is done in an equitable fashion.

The social worker is thus responsible for rationing his own resources, a task that requires the capacity to plan the use of time in the most effective way possible. In ideal circumstances, he would be able to allocate to clients exactly the right amount of time and attention that would lead to the resolution of their difficulties, but quite apart from the impracticability of this in the light of scarcity of resources, it is doubtful whether there is any way of estimating the needs of clients in such precise terms. In practice, such planning has to be done on a day-to-day or weekly basis, allowing for the possibility of rapid changes in demand that arise from the unpredictable crises of life. Compromise between the ideal and reality is thus always necessary, but this process is greatly eased if the social worker is methodical in his organisation of work. Methodical organisation requires the employment of two important skills. The first is the ability to place work tasks in an order of priority, to enable decisions to be made about what should be done first and what can safely be left until a later stage or day. Although this point may seem self-evident, it is surprising how many social workers appear to lack the capacity for logical thought about priorities and thus work in a state of confusion which at best implies haphazard service to clients and at worst may lead to neglect that becomes a national scandal, when someone in need is not visited and tragic consequences ensue. The second organisational skill is the ability to plan a daily programme of work that is economical and efficient, insofar as the demands on the social worker permit. This involves careful distribution of time between office-based work, whether client contact or administration, and activities elsewhere, such as home visits and meetings. It also involves the planning of travelling time in such a way that journeys are not unnecessarily duplicated. The use of a system of appointments is of enormous assistance in the planning of a work programme, which should be recorded in a diary to which constant reference may be made. Time must always be allowed for unexpected emergencies, but this can be incorporated in diary planning, which if conscientiously carried out often leads to a reduced feeling of pressure and greater job satisfaction for the social worker.

Reports and Records. It has already been stated that social workers require skill in the spoken word, both in dealings with clients and with the staff of other agencies, including those such as the courts which operate in public and therefore demand a highly developed capacity for verbal communication. This capacity is also vitally important in using the telephone, which is of increasing importance in all kinds of transactions, both with clients and in the environment. As well as these important matters, however, it is essential that social workers should be skilled in the use of the written word. They are required to write letters, both to clients and to other agencies and organisations, in which they must match tone and content to the recipient, using varying degrees of formality and warmth of expression. Furthermore, they have to submit reports to courts, clinics, hospitals and other organisations, in which they provide comprehensive information about clients, often including an assessment of their current situation and indications of their future prospects. Such report writing requires thought and care if the result is to play an effective part in the social work process. The Streatfeild Committee on the

Business of the Criminal Courts[3] suggested that all information contained in reports to the high courts should be 'relevant, reliable and comprehensive' and this seems a good basis for the construction of all reports written by social workers. It is also helpful if reports are written in a chronological sequence in terms of life history and set out under sub-headings where appropriate. They should be free of jargon that is likely to provide an obstacle to understanding. In most cases it is also vital that clients should know what is contained in reports about them and it is often possible to involve them actively in the construction of the report. Social workers sometimes lack honesty in withholding information from clients and although there are occasionally circumstances in which such action may be justifiable, widespread secrecy can only lead to suspicion and lack of trust that is counter-productive in the social work process.

Besides writing reports, all social workers are required by their employers to keep records of their work. Foremost among these are case records in which there is usually some form of ongoing account giving details of each contact and communication between social worker and client, together with an occasional summary of events and progress. The probation and after-care service has a standardised record form that is used in England and Wales and includes provision for quarterly assessments as well as day-to-day details. In other agencies, practice varies and the importance of regular summaries is often under-estimated, with the result that the continuing process of assessment receives inadequate support on paper. Case records are usually said to exist for a number of reasons: they provide some proof to employers that work has been done, though obviously they may easily be falsified; they are useful when one social worker succeeds another and needs to grasp the essentials of cases quickly; and they are of some help to the social worker in analysing his work, particularly when he comes to review intervention over a period of time, for which memory would be unreliable. It has also been suggested that records may be useful in the context of research but although they have served this purpose from time to time, they suffer from serious limitations, including lack of standardisation and inconsistency between workers, both of which raise doubts about their validity.

The preparation of records and reports requires time for thought and sometimes for discussion with colleagues and superiors. These factors are growing in significance as social workers attempt to work in an increasing number of dimensions. The recording of work with individuals and families seems relatively simple when compared with the complexities presented by group interaction or community involvement, for neither of which satisfactory systems of recording have yet been developed. It is especially important that effective recording systems for new or experimental types of social work should be developed, because these serve one of the original purposes of records, their use in teaching and in transmitting knowledge and skills to the profession as a whole. The creation of new systems of recording requires a team approach, with senior staff taking special responsibilities for innovation.

Social workers are also involved in the keeping of various kinds of statistics. They may be asked for information on a regular basis, including details of work-loads and of miles travelled and expenses incurred in the course of their work. Social workers are prone to regard statistics as uninteresting, yet their work places in their possession a great deal of factual information about individuals, families and communities, which can sometimes be used in promoting changes in social policy. On occasions, it may be necessary for them to collect figures specifically for the purpose of providing evidence of need, for example for play facilities for children or for a club for the recovering mentally ill. Community workers, in particular, find themselves involved in survey activities of varying degrees of complexity and they may need to acquire special skills in such aspects as sampling techniques and questionnaire construction. There is always a danger of doing surveys for their own sake and their value is often further limited by the over-exposure of their clients to the technique from other sources, such as politics and commerce. On the other hand, a survey that is carefully constructed and directed to specific ends is often a valuable part of a programme of intervention, particularly if it demonstrates the reality of hitherto unnoticed need.

Confidentiality. The existence of records in social work agencies raises certain ethical issues, notably the question of confidentiality and the extent to which clients are made aware of what is contained in the files. It seems important that in talking to social workers clients should be aware that what they say is not necessarily a secret between them alone. Most clients are likely to accept that, like doctors, social workers need to keep notes on them as a means of reminding them of the issues involved and of assisting them in the process of providing help. They are also likely to be able to understand that any such records belong to the agency rather than to the individual social worker and that consequently other members of staff may see what is contained in them. It is normal for social workers to indicate to clients that except in such situations as enquiries for the courts, no information given by them will be passed to anyone outside the agency without their permission, thus providing a certain safeguard in relation to the office files.

It seems possible that social workers are sometimes more concerned about confidentiality than are their clients, whose life style has perhaps not accustomed them to hiding very much from other people. Nevertheless, clients have a right to expect that what they say to a social worker will not be passed on to neighbours or friends as gossip and in some situations, such as work with marital pairs, the preservation of confidentiality is a key issue, it being essential for each partner to feel free to speak to the social worker without reservation or fear that their spouse will be acquainted with what has been said. A further complication occurs when clients put social workers in possession of information that is embarrassing or incriminating. It may well be a sign of positive progress that such a disclosure occurs, but the social worker may as a result be left to resolve the dilemma of whether to reveal the information to someone else by including it in the official record or speaking to a colleague, or whether simply to retain it unrecorded for his own use. When criminal matters are concerned, many would say that there can be no dilemma, since it is the responsibility of all citizens to ensure that offenders are apprehended, but there can be no hard-and-fast rule even about this, particularly as such disclosures often relate to the past rather than the present and some may represent fantasy rather than reality. In general, the social worker must examine his conscience and use his judgement in these extreme cases, balancing responsibility to the client against the needs of other members of his family and of society in general.

The problem of the extent to which clients are aware of what is written about them in the files of social work agencies has already been discussed in connection with the writing of reports. Records which are factual present few problems, but most also contain a certain amount of speculative material, some of it tentative, which represents the social worker's analysis of the current situation and which may well be modified by subsequent events. Most social workers would no doubt find it embarrassing if they had to reveal all such material to their clients but the question arises of whether it is justifiable to keep records of this type. In addition to the social worker's assessments, records sometimes contain factual information of which clients are unaware and which it might not be helpful to disclose to them. For example, some people who are illegitimate do not know this fact and it might not help them to reveal it, at any rate not at the time when the social worker first acquires the information. In hospital social work records, the medical diagnosis often appears, but this is usually restricted information which no one but the doctor may reveal to the patient, however strongly the social worker feels that it should be divulged. The conclusion must be that as far as possible clients who wish it should be allowed to know what is written about them in the official records of a social work agency, but as a safeguard there must be the right to withhold information when it is genuinely believed to be wise to do so.

Decisions. Administration also involves skill in taking decisions. Although decisions in relation to clients are usually seen as professional in nature, they also have important administrative components related to the allocation and use of resources. Thus, although the decision to use a particular strategy of intervention sometimes has no consequences outside the relationship between social worker and client and can be taken in isolation, other approaches involve the use of resources such as money, material aid and day and residential care facilities, which have wider repercussions. In taking such decisions, the social worker may believe that he has a strong case for assisting a client in a particular way, but as was pointed out in Chapter 8 in discussing the mobilisation of community resources, he is often in a competitive situation and cannot guarantee success every time.

The most important foundation for effective decision-making is comprehensive assessment, in which the issues and possibilities are clearly demonstrated. Once the nature of the decision required is indicated, it may be necessary to use skill in marshalling evidence to produce a convincing case, which requires the employment of persuasive powers in presentation. Some social workers go beyond this and involve themselves in lobbying and other work in the background which is likely to produce the kind of decision required. This technique can be very useful in community work and is also employed at managerial level in social work agencies and there seems no reason why it should not be used judiciously to obtain decisions that favour individual clients and families. There are problems of conflict of loyalty here that the social worker needs to be able to tolerate, since for the most part they are incapable of resolution. Thus decisions that favour one individual or family can rarely be made without affecting others, whether clients, colleagues, employers or society as a whole, but this is a factor that is endemic in social work and cannot be avoided.

The taking of a decision helps to clarify the direction in which a case is proceeding. It cannot always be taken in the light of the full facts about a situation, since they are rarely available in their entirety either to the social worker or to the client. This means that many decisions are informed guesses or compromises that are far from the ideal. For these reasons it is particularly important that as far as possible clients should participate fully in decisions that affect their lives, particularly when major changes are involved. Thus any decision to leave home and enter residential care must, except in real emergencies, be based on careful thought and discussion, accompanied where possible by a chance for the client to sample the residential facilities on a trial basis, with freedom to leave if not satisfied. Even if decisions have to be taken in a hurry, as when children or mentally disordered adults are removed from home in a crisis situation, it is essential that they be given a thorough explanation of what is happening to them, however limited their capacity to understand appears to be. Relatives should also be fully involved in the discussions that lead to the decision. Speedy decisions are part of the social worker's daily experience, but he should always try to organise his work so that clients and their families have adequate time to prepare for the consequence of a major decision, preferably through helping them to make it themselves, rather than imposing it on them.

Social Work Skills

It should be clear from the preceding discussion that social workers must possess a wide range of skills to enable them to practise effectively. The following table is a summary of those aspects of skill which have been discussed in this book, but it is recognised that readers may wish to add others that they have identified for themselves.

TABLE III: AREAS OF SKILL

Relationship Skills	
1. *Management of Relationships*	2. *Creation and Use of Relationships*
Initiation	Individuals
Maintenance and development	Pairs
Termination and transfer	Families
Crisis intervention	Groups
	People in the environment
	Organisations in the environment

TABLE III: AREAS OF SKILL (*cont.*)

Transactional Skills

1. *Communication*	2. *Overcoming Problems*
Observing	Language
Receiving	Irrationality
Listening	Apathy
Interpreting for oneself	Silences
Responding	Mental disorders
Questioning	Alien cultures
Interpreting to others	Alien value systems
Summarising	Intuition
Planning action	

3. *Management of Transactions*
   - Dimension(s)
   - Venue
   - Frequency
   - Length

Organisational Skills

1. *Agency Membership*	2. *Management*
Teamwork	Clerical staff
Collaboration within the agency	Ancillary workers
Collaboration with other agencies	Volunteers
Using consultation	Promotion of organisational change
Using supervision	Management and development of own resources
	Work load management—planning of priorities and work programme

3. *Administration*
   - Reports and records
   - Statistics and data collection
   - Preservation of confidentiality
   - Taking decisions

13

Skills and Methods in a Professional Context

The model of social work outlined in this book is one which presents it as a process requiring the use of a range of skills in the assessment of need, in the choice and implementation of suitable strategies of intervention, and in the evaluation of the work done. The basic skills in relationships, transactions and working in an organisational context are required by all social workers, whatever their tasks and functions and thus they constitute a common core of expertise. Skills are derived in part from the personal attributes of each social worker, but they are also developed through education, training and experience. This means that there are clearly different levels of skill among social workers, according to individual characteristics, capacity and opportunity for learning, and length of experience. It also means that skills may develop on a differential basis, with the result that some social workers are highly competent in some areas of work and less able in others. This is frequently to be observed in those social workers whose relationships with clients are excellent but whose administrative work is barely adequate to meet the requirements of the agency. It is the argument of this book that effective social work requires competence in all aspects of skill, but the degree of expertise needed is also dependent on the nature of the task and the function of the particular worker.

The nature of the task in social work springs from the needs of the client and the assessment that is made at the point at which contact is established with the social work agency. As was indicated in Chapter 12, intake work and initial assessments demand high levels of knowledge and skill and there are good arguments in favour of using experienced workers in this capacity. If contact between client and agency is to be maintained over a period of time, however, the level of skill required depends to a large extent on the nature of the strategies of intervention to be employed. It may be argued that some strategies require less skill than others and may thus be used by staff with less knowledge and experience in appropriate cases. Among those requiring less skill, it would be possible to include the provision of information and advice and the use of oversight. In contrast, it might be thought that strategies such as behaviour modification or creating an appropriate psychological environment would demand a high degree of skill. Attempts to differentiate levels of skill have been a contributory factor in the introduction of new types of staff in social work agencies, their role being seen as one of relieving social workers of tasks requiring less highly developed skill. Welfare assistants and ancillary workers are thus expected to carry out routine duties of a relatively straightforward nature, with clear instructions to report to a social worker the appearance of anything unusual or possibly problematic. The argument for using volunteers is generally a little different in that it emphasises that they may contribute to the welfare of clients in ways not open to the paid social worker, such as through friendship, more frequent contact and a higher degree of personal involvement than is usual in a professional relationship. Nevertheless, the volunteer, like the welfare assistant, is expected to be alert in noticing untoward developments and referring them to the appropriate social worker.

Although this kind of differentiation is theoretically appealing, it is not easily implemented in practice. The needs of clients rarely fit the categorisations of social workers, so that there is always the likelihood that a welfare assistant or voluntary worker will find himself drawn beyond prescribed tasks into work requiring greater skill, which he may or may not possess. On the positive side, it may be said that all experience provides learning opportunities and that demands for assistance that go beyond a worker's prescribed role may help him to develop new skills and capacities.

In some cases such an experience may add to the source of recruitment to professional social work. On the other hand, if a welfare assistant or volunteer fails to seek more expert assistance when it is needed, clients may receive inadequate or inappropriate service. Some would argue that the needs of clients are so varied and liable to change that it is inappropriate for assistance to be provided by anyone other than a professional social worker, who possesses the full range of skills, but that denies the reality that there are many tasks in social work which can be prescribed with clarity, which do not demand a high level of interpersonal skill and which it is therefore appropriate to allocate to ancillary staff. Escort duties and many types of practical assistance come under this heading, sometimes involving the use of skills that social workers are not normally expected to possess, such as carrying out electrical repairs or interior decorating.

The needs of clients, therefore, indicate that although assessment must be carried out on a comprehensive basis, further intervention may sometimes be assigned to a worker of relatively limited skill and experience, performing mainly prescribed tasks. This aspect can be seen as forming one extreme of a continuum at the opposite end of which lies the provision of highly skilled assistance of a specialised nature. This latter type of specialisation is distinctive from the functional kind relating to agency responsibilities, discussed in Chapter 12. It is a specialisation relating to the nature of intervention, in which one particular approach is used in dealing with a wide range of problems. Examples of this are the use of psychotherapy or behaviour modification as distinctive and specialised strategies of intervention. Although it is the argument of this book that social workers generally require a wide range of skills in intervention, there is a good case for some of them developing specialist interests in certain specific strategies. A specialist of this kind is more likely than a general social worker to be able to study thoroughly the relevant literature and research relating to his particular interest and this, together with the greater depth and intensity of experience gained by concentrating on a clearly defined area of work, increases his ability to intervene effectively, especially in complex situations. In some instances, specialists may act in a pioneering role, developing a new form of service which eventually becomes part of the repertoire of his general social work colleagues. The community work field provides many examples of this, such as the interest in neighbourhood work that has begun to develop among the staff of area social services offices and the initial work performed by specialists in the probation and after-care service in connection with the community service scheme, in the expectation that the responsibility will eventually be spread more widely. It is also important for social workers to develop specialisation in its own right as a means of improving the service available to the client on a regular basis. Thus certain social workers may wish to specialise in working with groups and others in community work. Through concentration on specific types of work and on the enhancement of distinctive skills, the practice of social work is developed and refined until it reaches a stage where its methodology must be re-interpreted. Any analysis of skills and methods in social work, including the one in this book, must be subject to reformulation if it is to remain relevant to the nature of the tasks and objectives in practice.

Professionalism

It should be clear from the contents of this book that the view that any well-meaning person can be a social worker is no longer tenable. Attributes of personality are emphasised throughout the text, but they must be accompanied by knowledge and skill, acquired through training and experience, if the complexities of the social system and of individual, family and community needs are to be mastered in the process of initiating effective intervention. Moreover, social work is always facing new situations and new problems. It has moved from a stance of primary concern with the rescue of social casualties to a comprehensive approach to prevention and the promotion of social welfare. In the future, it seems likely that more attention will have to be given to tackling the problems that arise in a multi-generational and multi-racial society, in which the prevalence of conflictual behaviour is more apparent. This will undoubtedly give rise to major moral and ethical issues about the function of social work in society and the extent to which it should be involved in promoting conflict rather than consensus.

Social work is thus not an easy occupation in which work can be done without regard to social and moral consequences. In facing the dilemmas inherent in their occupation, social workers find support and strength in the membership of a common body, but the question arises of whether it is proper to regard this as a profession. Many social workers consider it essential to attain the kind of professional status that would place them on an equal footing with doctors, lawyers and other long-established callings. To others, the idea of professionalism is anathema, because it appears to create an insuperable boundary between them and their clients in a field of work which they believe demands relationships of equality in which the integrity of all participants is acknowledged, together with the reality that the person who does most to solve his problem is the client himself.

Arguments about whether social work is a true profession are largely semantic. One writer[1] resolves the difficulty by including social work in a group of semi-professions, such as teaching and nursing. This seems to accord well with the reality of the situation, since not all of the attributes commonly associated with professionalism are to be found in social work. Greenwood[2] describes these as a systematic body of theory, professional authority, community sanction, a regulative code of ethics and a distinctive culture. Social work as yet lacks a systematic body of theory, being dependent on knowledge derived from other subjects of study, though it can claim to synthesise it in a unique way. It can also be claimed that research studies are beginning to contribute to the creation of a body of theory, but it is still far from developed. Social work also lacks a regulative code of ethics, though attempts have been made from time to time to remedy this.[3] On the other hand, social workers undoubtedly possess professional authority that springs from their knowledge, skill and experience in social intervention. They have the sanction of the community in the sense that it is the community that gives them their powers and the right to do their work, though many social workers would like a formal system of registration to be introduced as a more effective means of control. They also have a distinctive culture in the form of professional associations that are striving to increase their influence in both policy and practice. In this book, social work has been described throughout as professional not only for all of these reasons, but also because it is through the professional orientation of the social worker that the client can be assured of protection from attempts at manipulation and coercion and of the right to receive skilled help and guidance that is carefully matched to the nature of his needs.

References

Introduction

1. *Report of the Committee on Local Authority and Allied Personal Social Services*; HMSO, 1968.
2. 'The Community Work Group', *Current Issues in Community Work*, p. 107; Routledge and Kegan Paul, 1973.

Chapter One The Basis of Social Work

1. Robinson, J. N. G., 'The Dual Commitment of Social Work', *British Journal of Social Work*, Vol. 2, No. 4, pp. 471–80; 1972.
2. Leighton, N., 'The Act of Understanding', *British Journal of Social Work*, Vol. 3, No. 4, pp. 509–24; 1973.
3. The terms 'residential centre' and 'day centre' are used in this book in preference to 'home' or 'establishment' in keeping with the views expressed in the Report of the Working Party on Education for Residential Work, *Residential Work is a Part of Social Work*, published by the Central Council for Education and Training in Social Work, 1973.

Chapter Two The Social Worker's Clientèle

1. Wootton, B., *Social Science and Social Pathology*, Chapter Nine; George Allen and Unwin, 1959.
2. Goetschius, G. W., *Working with Community Groups*; Routledge and Kegan Paul, 1969.
3. Briggs, D., 'De-clienting Social Work', *Social Work Today*, Vol. 3, No. 21, pp. 3–6; 1973.

4. Lees, R., *Politics and Social Work*; Routledge and Kegan Paul, 1972.
5. See, for example, Hardiker, P., 'Problem Definition: an Interactionist Approach' in Jehu, D., Hardiker, P., Yelloly, M., and Shaw, M., *Behaviour Modification in Social Work*, pp. 99–125; Wiley-Interscience, 1972.
6. Young, M., and Willmott, P., *Family and Kinship in East London*; Routledge and Kegan Paul, 1957.
   Townsend, P., *The Last Refuge*; Routledge and Kegan Paul, 1964.
7. *Report of the Working Party on Social Workers in the Local Authority Health and Welfare Services*; HMSO, 1959.
8. Home Office, *Report on the Work of the Probation and After-Care Department, 1969–71*; HMSO, 1972.
9. *Report of the Committee on Local Authority and Allied Personal Social Services*; HMSO, 1968.
10. *Better Services for the Mentally Handicapped*; HMSO, 1971.
11. Parker, R. A., 'Social Administration and Scarcity: the Problem of Rationing', *Social Work (UK)*, Vol. 24, No. 2, pp. 9–14; 1967.
12. Marris, P., and Rein, M., *Dilemmas of Social Reform*; Routledge and Kegan Paul, 1967.

Chapter Three The Assessment of Social Situations

1. Richmond, M., *Social Diagnosis*; Russell Sage Foundation, 1917.
2. Sainsbury, E. E., *Social Diagnosis in Casework*; Routledge and Kegan Paul, 1970.
3. Leighton, N., 'The Act of Understanding', *British Journal of Social Work*, Vol 3, No. 4, pp. 509–24; 1973.
4. Reid, W. J., and Epstein, L., *Task-centered Casework*; Columbia University Press, 1972.
5. Cunningham, J., *Developments in Social Work*, Chapter Six; British Broadcasting Corporation, 1974.

Chapter Four Action and Evaluation

1. Reid, W. J., and Shyne, A. W., *Brief and Extended Casework*; Columbia University Press, 1969.
2. See, for example, Mayer, J. E., and Timms, N., *The Client Speaks*,

Working Class Impressions of Casework; Routledge and Kegan Paul, 1970.

Chapter Five Strategies of Social Intervention

1. Reid, W. J., and Shyne, A. W., *Brief and Extended Casework*; Columbia University Press, 1969.
2. Reid, W. J., and Epstein, L., *Task-centered Casework*; Columbia University Press, 1972.
3. Mayer, J. E., and Timms, N., *The Client Speaks. Working Class Impressions of Casework*; Routledge and Kegan Paul, 1970.
4. See, for example, Townsend, P., *The Last Refuge*; Routledge and Kegan Paul, 1964 *and* Goffman, E., *Asylums*; Anchor Books, 1961.
5. Bowlby, J., *Maternal Care and Mental Health*; WHO Monograph Series, 1951 *and* Ainsworth, M., *et al. Deprivation of Maternal Care: A Reappraisal of its Effects*; WHO Public Health Papers 14, 1962.
6. Roof, M., *A Hundred Years of Family Welfare. A Study of the Family Welfare Association (formerly Charity Organisation Society) 1869–1969*; Michael Joseph, 1972.
7. Hollis, F., *Casework: a Psychosocial Therapy*; Random House, 1964.
8. Perlman, H. H., *Social Casework: a Problem-solving Process*; University of Chicago Press, 1957.
9. Biestek, F. P., *The Casework Relationship*; Loyola University Press, 1957.
10. See, for example, Sinfield, A., *Which Way for Social Work?*; Fabian Tract 393, Fabian Society, 1969.
11. Bartlett, H., *The Common Base of Social Work Practice*, p. 101; National Association of Social Workers, New York, 1970.
12. Bartlett, op. cit., p. 109.
13. Bartlett, op. cit., p. 79.
14. Bartlett, op. cit., p. 79.
15. Younghusband, E., 'The Future of Social Work', *Social Work Today*, Vol. 4, No. 2, pp. 33–7; 1973.
16. See, for example, Goldstein, H., *Social Work Practice: a Unitary Approach*; University of South Carolina Press, 1973 *and* Pincus, A., and Minahan, A., *Social Work Practice: Model and Method*; F. E. Peacock Publishers, 1973.

Chapter Six Interpersonal Intervention (i) Providing and Enabling

1. Wootton, B., *Social Science and Social Pathology*, Chapter Nine, p. 296; George Allen and Unwin, 1959.
2. Mayer, J. E., and Timms, N., *The Client Speaks. Working Class Impressions of Casework*; Routledge and Kegan Paul, 1970.
3. Glover, E., *Probation and Re-education*; Routledge and Kegan Paul, 1949.
4. The common ground between social work and education is discussed in Clyne, P., *The Disadvantaged Adult. Educational and Social Needs of Minority Groups*; Longman, 1972.
   See also Department of Education and Science *Adult Education: a Plan for Development*; HMSO, 1973.
5. Hollis, F., *Casework: a Psychosocial Therapy*; Random House, 1964.
6. Examples may be found in Mitton, R., and Morrison, M., *A Community Project in Notting Dale*; Allen Lane, The Penguin Press, 1972.
7. Saunders, C., 'Death in Family: a Professional View', *British Medical Journal*, Vol. 1, p. 30; 1973.
8. Hollis, F., *Casework: a Psychosocial Therapy*; Random House, 1964.
9. Irvine, E. E., 'A New Look at Casework', Chapter Two of *New Developments in Casework*, compiled by Younghusband, E.; George Allen and Unwin, 1966.

Chapter Seven Interpersonal Intervention (ii) Influencing and Creating

1. See, for example, Jehu, D., *Learning Theory and Social Work*; Routledge and Kegan Paul, 1967.
2. Jehu, D., Hardiker, P., Yelloly, M., and Shaw, M., *Behaviour Modification in Social Work*, p. 70; Wiley-Interscience, 1972.
3. See, for example, Shaw, M., 'Ethical Implications of a Behavioural Approach', in Jehu, Hardiker, Yelloly and Shaw, op. cit., pp. 161–72.
4. Mayer, J. E., and Timms, N., *The Client Speaks. Working Class Impressions of Casework*; Routledge and Kegan Paul, 1970.
5. Storr, A., *The Integrity of the Personality*; Heinemann, 1960.

Chapter Eight Environmental Intervention

1. Stevenson, O., *Claimant or Client? A Social Worker's View of the Supplementary Benefits Commission*; George Allen and Unwin, 1973.
2. *Report of the Committee on Local Authority and Allied Personal Social Services*, Chapter Sixteen; HMSO, 1968.
3. Carter, D., and Barter, J., 'Climbing off the Fence', *Social Work Today*, Vol. 3, No. 10, pp. 4–6; 1972.
4. The National Community Development Project: Inter Project Report 1973; CDP Information and Intelligence Unit, 1974.

Chapter Nine Relationships in Social Work (i) Characteristics and Phases

1. Leighton, N., 'The Act of Understanding', *British Journal of Social Work*, Vol. 3, No. 4, pp. 509–24; 1973.
2. Caplan, G., *Principles of Preventive Psychiatry*; Basic Books, 1964.
3. Rapoport, L., 'The State of Crisis: Some Theoretical Considerations', *Social Service Review*, Vol. 36, No. 2, pp. 211–17; 1962.
4. Rapoport, op. cit.
5. Rapoport, op. cit.
6. Irvine, E. E., 'A New Look at Casework', Chapter Two, p. 46 of *New Developments in Casework* compiled by Younghusband, E.; George Allen and Unwin, 1966.

Chapter Ten Relationships in Social Work (ii) Clients and the Environment

1. See, for example, Bell, J. E., *Family Group Therapy*; Bookstall Publications, 1971; Scherz, F. H., 'Theory and Practice of Family Therapy', Chapter Six of *Theories of Social Casework*, edited by Roberts, R. W. and Nee, R. H., University of Chicago Press, 1971; and Younghusband, E., (Ed.) *Social Work with Families*, George Allen and Unwin, 1965.
2. Jordan, W., *The Social Worker in Family Situations*; Routledge and Kegan Paul, 1972. See also Jordan, W., *Client-Worker Transactions*; Routledge and Kegan Paul, 1970.

3. Halliwell, R., 'Time Limited Work with a Family at Point of Being Prosecuted for Child Neglect', *Case Conference*, Vol. 15, No. 9, pp. 343–48; 1969.

Chapter Eleven Transactions in Social Work

1. Central Council for Education and Training in Social Work, *Social Work. Residential Work is a Part of Social Work*, Report of the Working Party on Education for Residential Social Work, para. 41; 1973.

Chapter Twelve Organisational Skills

1. *Better Services for the Mentally Handicapped*; HMSO, 1971.
2. *Report of the Care of Children Committee*; HMSO, 1946.
3. *Report of the Interdepartmental Committee on the Business of the Criminal Courts*, para. 323; HMSO, 1961.

Chapter Thirteen Skills and Methods in a Professional Context

1. Etzioni, A., *The Semi-Professions and their Organisation: Teachers, Nurses and Social Workers*; The Free Press, 1969.
2. Greenwood, E., 'Attributes of a Profession', *Social Work (USA)*, Vol. 2, No. 3, pp. 45–55; 1957.
3. See, for example, British Association of Social Workers *Discussion Paper No. 2. A Code of Ethics for Social Work*; BASW, 1972.

Bibliography

Bartlett, H. M., *The Common Base of Social Work Practice*; National Association of Social Workers, New York, 1970.

Biestek, F. E., *The Casework Relationship*; Loyola University Press, 1957.

Briar, S. and Miller, H., *Problems and Issues in Social Casework*; Columbia University Press, 1971.

Calouste Gulbenkian Foundation, *Community Work and Social Change*; Longman, 1968.

The Community Work Group, *Current Issues in Community Work*; Routledge and Kegan Paul, 1973.

Etzioni, A., *Modern Organizations*; Prentice-Hall, 1964.

Hollis, F., *Casework: a Psychosocial Therapy*; Random House, 1964, and second edition 1972.

Jehu, D., *Learning Theory and Social Work*; Routledge and Kegan Paul, 1967.

Jehu, D., Hardiker, P., Yelloly, M., and Shaw, M., *Behaviour Modification in Social Work*; Wiley-Interscience, 1972.

Jordan, W., *Client-Worker Transactions*; Routledge and Kegan Paul, 1970.

Jordan, W., *The Social Worker in Family Situations*; Routledge and Kegan Paul, 1972.

Lees, R., *Politics and Social Work*; Routledge and Kegan Paul, 1972.

Leonard, P., *Sociology in Social Work*; Routledge and Kegan Paul, 1966.

Mayer, J. E. and Timms, N., *The Client Speaks. Working Class Impressions of Casework*; Routledge and Kegan Paul, 1970.

Monger, M., *Husband, Wife and Caseworker*; Butterworths, 1971.

Northen, H., *Social Work with Groups*; Columbia University Press, 1969.

Perlman, H. H., *Social Casework: a Problem-solving Process*; University of Chicago Press, 1957.

Plant, R., *Social and Moral Theory in Casework*; Routledge and Kegan Paul, 1970.

Reid, W. J. and Epstein, L., *Task-centered Casework*; Columbia University Press, 1972.

Reid, W. J. and Shyne, A. W., *Brief and Extended Casework*; Columbia University Press, 1969.

Roberts, R. W., and Nee, R. H., *Theories of Social Casework*; University of Chicago Press, 1971.

Rogers, C. R., *Encounter Groups*; Harper and Row, 1970.

Ruddock, R., *Roles and Relationships*; Routledge and Kegan Paul, 1966.

Sainsbury, E. E., *Social Diagnosis in Casework*; Routledge and Kegan Paul, 1970.

Smith, G., *Social Work and the Sociology of Organisations*; Routledge and Kegan Paul, 1970.

Spergel, I. A., *Community Problem Solving. The Delinquency Example*; University of Chicago Press, 1969.

Storr, A., *The Integrity of the Personality*; Heinemann, 1960.

Timms, N., *The Language of Social Casework*; Routledge and Kegan Paul, 1968.

Timms, N., *Social Work. An Outline for the Intending Student*; Routledge and Kegan Paul, 1970.

Warham, J., *An Introduction to Administration for Social Workers*; Routledge and Kegan Paul, 1967.

Woodroofe, K., *From Charity to Social Work*; Routledge and Kegan Paul, 1962.

Younghusband, E., (ed.), *New Developments in Casework*; George Allen and Unwin, 1966.

Younghusband, E., (ed.), *Social Work and Social Values*; George Allen and Unwin, 1967.

Younghusband, E., (ed.), *Social Work with Families*; George Allen and Unwin, 1965.

Index